Thomas W. Segady

Values, Neo-Kantianism and the Development of Weberian Methodology

PETER LANG

New York · Bern · Frankfurt am Main · Paris

Library of Congress Cataloging-in-Publication Data

Segady, Thomas W.
 Values, neo-Kantianism, and the development of Weberian
methodology.

 (American university studies. Series V,
Philosophy ; vol. 41)
  Bibliography: p.
  Includes index.
  1. Weber, Max, 1864–1920—Contributions in
methodology.   2. Methodology—History—20th century.
I. Title.   II. Series: American university studies.
Series V, Philosophy ; v. 41.
B3361.Z7S44   1987   300′.1′8   87-4111
 ISBN 0-8204-0506-X
 ISSN 0739-6392

CIP-Kurztitelaufnahme der Deutschen Bibliothek

Segady, Thomas W.:
Values, Neo-Kantianism, and the development of
Weberian methodology / Thomas W. Segady. –
New York; Bern; Frankfurt am Main; Paris:
Lang, 1987.
 (American University Studies; Ser. 5,
 Philosophy; Vol. 41)
 ISBN 0-8204-0506-X

NE: American University Studies / 05

© Peter Lang Publishing, Inc., New York 1987

Printed by Weihert-Druck GmbH, Darmstadt, West Germany

Values, Neo-Kantianism, and the Development
of Weberian Methodology

American University Studies

Series V
Philosophy

Vol. 41

PETER LANG
New York · Bern · Frankfurt am Main · Paris

For Gayle

TABLE OF CONTENTS

Preface.. ix

Introduction: The Problem of Assessing Weber's
    Methodological Thought............................. 1

PART ONE: THE HISTORICAL DIMENSION OF
WEBER'S METHODOLOGY

Chapter 1 Early Research Efforts.................... 21

Chapter 2 The Methodenstreit and the
           Werturteilstreit......................... 39

Chapter 3 Later Stages in the Development of
           of Weber's Methodological Thought......... 61

PART TWO: TOWARD A WEBERIAN METHODOLOGICAL
PROGRAM FOR THE SOCIAL SCIENCES

Chapter 4 Methodology............................... 85

Chapter 5 Methodological Concepts................... 101

Chapter 6 Research Methods.......................... 117

Chapter 7 Conclusion: Significance of a Weberian
           Methodological Program.................... 127

Appendix A: German Quotes Translated in the Text..... 145

Appendix B: Glossary of Major Terms.................. 151

Appendix C: Concepts Explicated by Weber in the
            "Categories" Essay....................... 155

Bibliography... 157

Index.. 167

Preface

The task of understanding Weber's entire corpus--both
methodological and substantive--is a herculean one. To
argue, over and above this, that one has found the "central
theme" uniting Weber's works into a "coherent whole" would
be absurd. A prolonged, careful scrutiny of Weber's
writings reveals numerous fundamental confusions and
contradictions (although, as Nietzsche reminds us, this in
itself is no fatal flaw). Thus, to assert that one is in
possession of the "truth" regarding Weber's meaning is
somewhat like the parable of the blind man grasping a part
of the elephant--we have grasped something, perhaps, but not
the whole truth. This has led, predictably, to what one
author has termed an entire cottage industry growing around
the problem of understanding Weber. The present effort,
while admittedly part of that industry, also hopes to
establish some ground for constructing a methodology based
on Weber's thought. Thus, it is "Weberian," but makes no
claim that it represents the "true" understanding of Weber.

One positive consequence of this cottage industry is
that we are beginning to understand that there are deeper
and more precise understandings of Weber, but that no final,
definitive statement is possible. The second, and most
important consequence, of this renewed intensive study of
Weber's works is that we are finding that this is one
"classic" mind that remains capable constantly of unlocking

new possibilities for contemporary thought in the social sciences. The message that Weber has been increasingly effective in bringing to the attention of social scientists is a critical awareness of not only how research in the social sciences should proceed, but why it must proceed thus and not otherwise if the meanings inherent underlying social life are to be fully understood.

INTRODUCTION: THE PROBLEM OF ASSESSING WEBER'S METHODOLOGY

The preeminence of Max Weber's standing in the ranks of sociologists scarcely requires documentation. Strauss (1953:36) has exclaimed that Weber "is the greatest social scientist of our century." This pronouncement has echoed across the most divergent lines within the discipline. Authors with such diverse perspectives as Parsons (1949), Winckelmann (1964), Gerth and Mills (1975), Schuetz (1964), Runciman (1972), Kaesler (1979), and Collins (1980), have offered praise of Weber's numerous contributions. Bogart (1977:1) has provided a distinct summary statement:

> Max Weber's work is recognized by the majority of sociologists as the most important attempt yet to elaborate the foundations for the science of society. Weber's definition of the nature and scope of sociological inquiry has dominated all subsequent discussion of the matter. His formulations are...accorded a respect far exceeding that given any other classical theorist, including his native countryman, Simmel, and the acknowledged master, Durkheim.

The recognition of the value of Weber's efforts has continued to increase; Weber has been quoted more often, and used as a fundamental source, than either Marx or Freud (Cahnman, 1979). One recent documentation of the literature lists a collection of over 2,300 titles of books and journal articles related to various aspects of Weber's writings. Roth and Schluchter (1979) have discovered that during the past decade, over 100 summaries and critiques of Weber's thought have been published each year, and this number has steadily been increasing.

However, this broadly-based acclaim of Weber's works has been accorded largely to his substantive efforts, rather than the methodological treatises. Butts (1977:236) has remarked that there has been "something of a paradox surrounding the incorporation of Weber's approach into modern sociology. [His] methodological rules are seen as quite out of date, or regarded as a 'pioneering effort,' a euphemism which damns with faint praise." While Weber's major substantive works have been translated almost entirely into English, Roth (1975:367) has noted that at least until 1975, only about half of Weber's methodological writings had been accessible to readers in English.[1] The reasons for this are numerous. Some, perhaps, stem from Weber himself, who exclaimed (1909a, 1949, 1975b), that methodology should occupy a status of lesser importance than substantive problems. Also, there is the frequent complaint that Weber's methodological writings were fragmentary, and never constituted a systematic whole (Abel, 1929; Bennion, 1933; Shils, 1949; Bruun, 1972; Torrance, 1974; Burger, 1976;

_____

[1] Only very recently have new, important methodological works by Weber been available in translation. For example, Huff (1984:18) has remarked that: "The recent translations of Roscher and Knies and Critique of Stammler mark a new beginning in the understanding of Weber's methodological thought."

Bogart, 1977; Heckmann, 1979; Tenbruck, 1980).

Further, Weber's methodological writings, often polemical in nature, were loosely composed in a style that has been characterized as "redundant, serpentine, bewildering, and occasionally even mysterious" (Oakes, 1975:8). Gilbert (1976:23) has remarked that: "Weber's methodological writings are so dense that only those possessed, in good Weberian form, by some Calvinist demon are willing to wade through them."

Thus, although summaries and critiques of Weber's most accessible methodological works abound, there have been few attempts to develop a systematic Weberian methodology based on the entirety of Weber's methodological corpus. Roth and Schluchter (1979:2), for example, have remarked that: "Many publications have dealt with the feasibility of interpretive sociology and the logical status of ideal types, but few writers have addressed Weber's actual research practice." This book constitutes one attempt to understand Weber's methodological corpus, and to examine the question: How could social science be possible using the basic elements that Weber provided? Or, as Sprondel et al. (1970:10) have asked: ["How could a general theory of sociological action be conceived that, at the same time, is adequately 'Weberian' in spirit?" A] Unfortunately, this question has largely been ignored.

It is suggested that systematization and refinement of Weber's methodology can be accomplished through two fundamental procedures: first, by developing an excursus detailing Weber's methodological writings and their historical context; and secondly, through a restructuring of his methodological corpus into analytically distinct, yet functionally meaningful units. This basic division--an historical account, and the restructuring of Weber's methodological thought--is reflected in the two major sections of the book. Thus, the attempt to develop a response to this question begins by tracing the lines of development and influences on Weber's thought, identifying his objectives in terms of this development, and finally, developing a methodological program that is consistent with his intent.

The purpose, then, is twofold: first, to provide a contribution to the history of sociology; and secondly, to establish a basis for the development of methodological procedures corresponding to Weber's postulates. Toward this end, evidence of Weber's intent will be provided by translating portions of previously untranslated writings by Weber. These quotes from previously untranslated German sources have been translated in the text, placed in brackets, and followed by an upper-case letter. The original German quotes corresponding to the letters are presented in Appendix "A". Additionally, a glossary of the central terms necessary for an understanding of Weber's methodology is presented in Appendix "B".

CRITICISMS OF WEBER'S METHODOLOGY

Even for those willing to confront Weber's prose, there are several issues to be addressed if understanding and systematization of a Weberian methodological program are to be obtained. Four general sources of critiques of Weber's methodology have surfaced. The first two--the critique of Weber's alleged "decisionism;" and what has been termed the "cumulative science argument"--are critiques of Weber's status within contemporary sociology. The second two sources of criticism are primarily concerned with the problems associated with translation and interpretation, and the problems inherent within the internal structure of Weber's social science method. Together, these critiques form the central concerns regarding the understanding of Weber's methodological intent, and they underscore the reason for the paucity of attempts to evaluate Weber's methodological contribution to current sociology.

The "Cumulative Science" Argument

Perhaps the most pervasive controversey surrounding Weber's potential contribution to contemporary sociology is whether the "classic" thinkers have lost their relevance in a discipline that has made--or at least has claimed to have made--considerable advances in both theory and research.

This argument is best summarized by Whitehead's (1959:162) assertion that "a science which hesitates to forget its founders is lost." Gibbs (1966) has stated categorically that those sociologists who have engaged in "ancestor worship" by adhering to the classical thinking of the "masters" (he labels these Weber, Pareto, Marx, and Durkheim), condemn the discipline to the incoherence and inconsistencies that often characterized the works of these thinkers. In the case of Weber, Bruun (1972:5) has remarked that:

> [Weber's] thought has been commented on, developed, modified, and attacked so often, and in so many different contexts, that Weber himself seems to vanish behind a mountain of references and commentaries.

This practice, rather than leading to any meaningful analysis of Weber's methodology, has often doomed his works to a role that becomes secondary to the interests of the authors who purportedly have sought to clarify his position. The eventual effect of this has been, ipso facto, the realization of Gibbs' assertion (cf. Giddens, 1976). Kaufman (1976:35) has termed this practice "exegetical thinking," whereby "...in one way or another, one assigns authority to a text, raising it above criticism, then reads one's thoughts into them [and] gets them back endowed with authority." This practice in relation to Weber's works has been widely noted (Bershady, 1973; Butts, 1977).

With respect to Weber's thought, two fundamental questions are raised by the cumulative science critique: To what extent should the classical writings belong to the corpus of contemporary sociology; and what kinds of contributions can they make to a discipline that has become more refined and oriented to the explanation of specific, concrete tasks that have become defined largely in terms of a quantitative form of empiricism? Certainly, the answer does not lie in the "lumping fallacy" exhibited by Gibbs' assessment, but through a considered analysis of each of the classical works. The claim cannot be made, as even Weber (1904 in 1949:104) suggested, that sociology is condemned to "eternal youth;" rather, a careful judgement must be made regarding the contributions of each individual author to the progress of the field as a whole.

Unfortunately, with many of Weber's works this task has proven to be exceedingly difficult. In Hegel's words, a great thinker not only condemns later authors to interpret him, but also to reconstruct his intellectual genealogy. Few sociologists, however, may claim the extensive eclectic education in law, history, economics, and philosophy that Weber incorporated into the fabric of his social thought. Marianne Weber (1975:676), for example, has stated that: "Weber's theory of concepts presupposes a comparative mastery of history because it is not derived from major terms or principles, as speculative systems are, but is directly evolved from the concrete factual material and composed inductively." Weber was considered an expert in jurisprudence, political economy, history, and comparative religion several years before he also became interested in sociology as a separate discipline (Bogart, 1977; Brand, 1979). This underscores Ritzer's (1975) observation that while Weberian scholars continue to exist in abundance (i.e., those who provide commentary on his works), there are no practicing "Weberians;" and Alexander's (1983) comment that no interpretive literature is more contradictory than the Weberian one.

Further, comparisons with other "masters" have produced little new knowledge that might extend the relevance of Weber's methodological works in contemporary sociology. Weber's thought has been linked to that of the neo-Hegelians (Martindale, 1959; Robertson, 1975; Giddens, 1978); Kant (Barker, 1980; Marianne Weber, 1975); several of the neo-Kantians (Lorenzen, 1970; Oakes, 1975; Collins, 1975; Brand, 1979); the German physiologist von Kries (Burger, 1976; Turner, 1983); Marx (Mueller, 1979; Zeitlin, 1973; Loewith, 1970; Gerth and Mills, 1975; Collins, 1980); Simmel (Tenbruck, 1959; Mueller, 1979); Troeltsch and Jellinek (Nelson, 1975; Robertson, 1975; Bendix and Roth, 1971); Nietzsche (Fleischmann, 1964; Coser, 1971; Mommsen, 1977a; Oakes, 1982); Dilthey (Hodges, 1949; Bruun, 1972); and Toennies (Bendix, 1962).

By themselves, however, these comparisons have accomplished little for two fundamental reasons. First, they have been effectively countered, in many instances, by other authors: Mommsen (1977b:6) has argued that Weber had "little in common with the historicism of the Hegelians;" and Brand (1979:6) has remarked that the attempt "...to picture Weber as the executor of a program suggested by Nietzsche is nothing less than preposterous." Bendix and Roth (1971), as well as Schluchter (1979), have contended that comparisons of Weber's works with the Marxists have largely been tendentious. For example, much of The Protestant Ethic was delivered by Weber in a series of lectures at the end of his life, under the title: "A Positive Critique of the Marxist Theory of History;" and its stated intention was to provide a critique of Marx's "historical materialism" (cf. Mommsen, 1977b:378). Further, Roth (1980:cii) has commented that: "There is no indication that Toennies' work was a major influence on Weber's intellectual development, and Economy and Society appears partly in opposition to it" (cf. Bendix, 1962:476).

Moreover, comparisons of Weber with other authors, even when valid, are of limited utility. As Kaesler (1979:196) has stated:

> [Discussions and depictions of the "connection" between Weber and Marx, Weber and Simmel, Weber and Parsons, etc., must become replaced by a systematic effort to research the influence on Weber's thought. In this manner, the danger of "comparing the incomparable" can be avoided, as well as to better per-

ceive Weber's works by avoiding the tendency to dis-
tort him either as hero or as ideologue. B]

The task of discovering Weber's worth for contemporary sociology, then, cannot be limited to random comparisons of his works with those of other thinkers. Any attempt to discover the potential for extending Weber's works more firmly into the corpus of modern sociology must begin with Weber's unique method of understanding social reality, focusing on the external sources that are relevant in this regard.

The Decisionist Critique

The argument has repeatedly surfaced that Weber's methodology--despite his considerable efforts to the contrary--manifests a "veiled, value-bound dimension," which subordinates the role of the social sciences vis-a-vis the controlling interests of a society. This results in the pragmatically impotent practice of "decisionism," which Roth and Schluchter (1979:74) have defined as "decisional premises [that] follow from what is technically feasible (not vice versa), and leadership is reduced to administration." Oakes (1982:591) has argued that with decisionism "...ultimate values are rationally indefensible." Several authors (Marcuse, 1968:221-226; Habermas, 1971:81-90; Horkheimer, 1973:6; Mommsen, 1977a:83; Elias, 1982:107), have asserted that the result of Weber's "uncritical" emphasis on "value-freedom" necessarily leads to the inability of the social sciences to formulate problems and solutions independently of the "administrative-technical" concerns of the non-scientific groups constituting the dominant powers of the society. For example, Habermas (in Cerny, 1964:58) remarked that a Nazi apologist such as Carl Schmidt could be regarded as a legitimate disciple of Weber.

Criticisms of this nature are directed at the heart of Weber's epistemological position, and attempt to equate his methodological stance with that of naive positivism. Ironically, Weber spent considerable effort cautioning against letting the facts "speak for themselves" (Weber, 1949:12-13; 1978c:77). Weber's first essays on the problem of values in the social sciences were a result of his involvement in the Werturteilstreit, an intense debate over the necessity of the purposive incorporation of values into social science method. This widespread debate took place in Germany during the years immediately following the turn of the century.

However, even Weber's earliest writings (e.g., Weber, 1891; 1893b; 1895), exhibited a visible concern for maximizing the possibilities for decision-making in the practical sphere--the sphere of action that is 'value-related' (Wertbezogenheit)--through scientific evidence and cumulative knowledge (Stammer, 1965; Schluchter, 1971;

Burger, 1977). For example, against those who declared that economic _policy_ must become the foundation for a science of economics, Weber demonstrated that this course of action actually diminishes the available range of options. As Bruun (1972:56) has stated: "Weber shows that such a procedure only serves the purpose of evading the decision, either in the sense that (e.g.), "economic development" is made to justify _any_ policy, or by way of legitimating the right of the economically strongest power."

Those who have been critical of Weber's writings in this regard have created a "straw man" argument, and have ignored much of Weber's reasoning in both his methodological and substantive writings (cf. Stammer, 1965; Schluchter, 1979). As Burger (1977) has demonstrated, Weber's notion of the separation of values from science does not exclude either a rational discussion of values or their empirical investigation. Weber's intention was, rather, in the direction of providing the most complete source of scientific knowledge possible--including the consequences of this knowledge--for its competent and productive utilization in the sphere of practical activity.

Nevertheless, the decisionist critique contains some merit, as it indicates the necessity of renewing the discussion of Weber's methodological position vis-a-vis the problem of values. There have been attempts to explicate in detail Weber's excursus on values, as well as to provide summaries of the critiques of his position (Bruun, 1972; Lewis, 1975). However, it remains to be shown how Weber distinguished between universal values, cultural values, value-relevance, value judgements, value-interpretation and value freedom, and the consequences of these for his development of various methodological arguments.

Ignorance of these distinctions of the concept of "value" may lead to further errors in conceptualizing Weber's methodological intent. Many of these basic concepts were articulated in Weber's earliest writings (Roth, 1968; Bruun, 1972; Kaesler, 1979), and indicate the need (particularly on the part of English-speaking sociologists), for considering a wider range of Weber's efforts. For example, Weber (1891) clearly stated a value premise in his study of the impacts of Roman expansionism on the lower strata of Roman citizenry, as well as in his analysis (1893b) of the political consequences for the Junkers of the intrusion by Polish workers into the eastern Prussian frontier. Additionally, a series of critical essays written between 1903 and 1913 demonstrate Weber's ongoing struggle to resolve this problem within the social sciences (cf. Oakes, 1975). If the decisionist critique is to be answered, these sources must be more closely examined.

Interpretation and Translation

Also central to understanding the potential for furthering Weber's contribution to sociology are the correct interpretation and, in non-German sociology, the accurate translation of his works. While other German authors consciously wrote in a manner facilitating translation (e.g., Nietzsche), Weber, unfortunately, was not one of these. This has led, predictably, to widespread confusion regarding the precise meaning of his works, and even the procedures to be taken for providing translations of them. Gerth and Mills (1975)--in concurrence with most translators--state that the three principles of translation are: (1) provision of the complete transcript of the author's ideas; (2) imitation of the style of the original author; and (3) preservation of the "readability" of the original text. These same authors have also observed, however, that "the second and third demands are often disputable in translating German into English, and, in the case of Weber, they are quite debatable" (Gerth and Mills, 1975:v). Along with other authors (Oakes, 1975; Marianne Weber, 1975), Bendix (1962) has lamented that Weber's major themes often became obscured in the mass of notes, qualifications, and illustrations that characterized his style.

Further, Roth (1978:cii), has found that there are "difficulties" with Weber's writings, including the fact that "...Weber never wrote a well-wrought book." Translators have responded in various ways to these problems, ranging from Bruun's (1972) leaving entire passages in the original German, and Graber's (1981:147) assertion that: "Where we must choose between fidelity to a precise formulation and readability, the former must be given extra weight;" to Gerth and Mills' procedure of radically restructuring Weber's sentences, and excluding the copious footnotes almost entirely.

The general problem of understanding Weber's works in their translated form thus appears to reside in two specific areas: (1) those problems that are the direct result of Weber's writings (and thus shared, to some extent, by readers in all languages, including German); and (2) those inherent in the structure of the language itself. The assessment of the impact of these problems requires closer examination.

First, regarding the problems inherent in Weber's own writings, Bendix has complained that, ultimately, "no simplification of sentence structure, terminology, and paraphrasing can remedy the defects from which the original suffers" (Bendix, 1962:xxiii). Thus, the commission of errors by Weber may only be further exacerbated by the problems inherent in the process of translation. It is also quite possible that many of the ongoing quarrels between various Weberian critics and translators can be reduced to the contradictions in Weber's own writings.[2]

It is Weber's methodological writings in which this problem is most keenly felt, and this may have been transferred to his substantive works. This, to some extent, may be a contributing factor to the lack of contemporary researchers who utilize a Weberian methodological approach. For example, Burger (1976:111) has observed that:

> Giving a meaningful content the form of a judgement Weber calls "interpretation" (Deutung), or also "interpretive understanding" (deutendes Verstehen). An interpretation is the imposition (Zumutung) of a judgement in the sense of the acknowledgement of an empirical interrelationship as a validly understood one. Unfortunately, Weber often uses the terms "interpret" and "understand" synonymously, with the inevitable result of terminological and theoretical confusion on the part of the reader. Thus, he equates "empathy" and "re-experiencing" with "interpretive understanding," calls "interpretation" an "absolutely secondary category which has lost its home in the artificial world of science," calls "understanding" an "interpretive grasp" (deutendes Erfassung), but also says that there is understanding whose purpose is not to produce a theoretical interpretation.

Burger has concluded from this that Weber's precise meaning must, in every instance, be judged by the reader. The problems this inevitably engenders, however, does not contribute to the notion of Weber's corpus as consisting of a workable methodological program. This terminological ambiguity, coupled with a "...tortuous, even tortured,

---

[2] For example, Weber often substituted the term "Vergesellschaftung" for "Gesellschaft;" and, as Bendix and Roth (1971:214) have remarked: "There is no proper English equivalent of this word, and it is not exactly usual in German, either."

density of Weber's intellectual texture reflected in his language" (Bruun, 1972:vii), leads to a misunderstanding of Weber's finer methodological distinctions, which, however central to his thought, are often tenuous and uncertain at best.

Lack of a Systematic Methodology

The possibility for achieving an adequate comprehension of Weber's works, particularly his methodological writings, is thus beset with several obstacles that confront the social scientist not acquainted with Weber in the German original. As critiques, corrections, and elaborations of earlier efforts are made available, however, these problems are certain to diminish.

Another problem in grasping the intricacies of Weber's works that may not be dispensed with in this manner, is the lack of a systematic program. It has been suggested (Parsons, 1965; Bruun, 1972; Burger, 1976; Gilbert, 1976; Heckmann, 1979), that Weber's methodological writings were not fully developed, and relied on the works of authors as divergent as Kant and von Kries. Indeed, this assessment appears to be correct, as Weber himself stated:

> [The attempt to link several methodological perspec-
> tives into a systematic investigation, has been
> abandoned. The results of [their] logic will be
> used, but not extended... (Weber, 1968:146n. C]

The effort of restructuring Weber's thought into a unified whole, then, must necessarily extend beyond Weber's own efforts. Specifically, Weber's methodological stance was influenced by the important debates surrounding the Methodenstreit. The same Weber who (in Oakes, 1975) remarked that methodology should only be a concern when the theory has failed, confirmed in a letter to Rickert (1909), that conditions had "forced" him to become a methodologist. This shift in position indicates the strength of Weber's response to the "crisis of values" that appeared in the Verein at this time. Thus, a consideration of both Weber's reaction to the school led by Schmoller, as well as the more positive influence of the Baden School of neo-Kantianism, is necessary in order to reconstruct a Weberian methodology. This requires an analysis of Weber's link to the neo-Kantians. As Barker (1980:225) has suggested:

> [Weber's] intellectual development was bound up with such leading neo-Kantians as Wilhelm Windelband, Wilhelm Rickert, and Ernst Troeltsch. But surprisingly little attention has been paid in a multiplicity of intellectual biographies to the actual impact and the specific results of these influences.

The question of whether Weber's corpus constituted a completed work requiring only refinement and application must be answered in the negative. It is clear that the actual status of Weber's methodological writings lies at a midpoint between complete fragmentation and a totally unified statement, and that a systematization of his works is a necessary condition for the application of a Weberian methodological perspective. What is required, first, is an approach that incorporates the entire range of Weber's works, and entails a discussion of lines of development in his methodological thought. Secondly, it must be established that Weber's arguments are largely an extension of and critical response to several major thinkers of his period. An analysis of Weber's intellectual milieu is central to understanding the structure of his thought--the problems he considered critical and the solutions he thought possible. Bruun (1972:17) has summarized this point in relation to Weber's pivotal position on value-freedom:

> To explain why it was Weber, rather than another scholar, who came to explore the principle of value freedom in all its details, some reference is necessary to the circumstances under which it came to be formulated. From the point of view of the theoretical discussion of the principle, these circumstances are of no particular importance; but they form the background of its formulation and growth, and put it in its proper polemical context.

Similarly, Nelson (1975:270-271), in an analysis of Weber's major objectives, has remarked that: "...the chronological sequence of Weber's writings [proves] to be a critical prerequisite in the gathering of reference points needed for a valuable assessment of Weber's central purposes and achievements."

Finally, critiques of Weber's methodology, particularly in relation to his concepts of the ideal type (Euken, 1951; Schweitzer, 1964; Lazarsfeld and Oberschall, 1965; Blau and

Meyer, 1971; Bendix and Roth, 1971; Diamant, 1962; Lopreato and Alston, 1970; Machlup, 1960; Runciman, 1972), and Verstehen (Abel, 1948; Munch, 1957; Tucker, 1965; Baar, 1967; Wax, 1967; Warriner, 1969; Leat, 1972; Markovic, 1972; Munch, 1975; Burger, 1977; Oakes 1982), mandate that any effort to refine Weber's method into a workable program must be sensitive to the legitimate concerns raised by these critiques.

Thus the attempt in this book is to move beyond a purely "synoptic" review of Weber's methodology, toward the development of a Weberian methodology that is consistent with Weber's objectives in outlining a course of inquiry for the social sciences. Given the conscious changes, as well as the inconsistencies and contradictions of Weber's thought, it is impossible to contend that this methodological model is what Weber would have formulated as a systematic methodology. It is possible, however, to establish reasoned judgements regarding his intent based on an interpretation of the central tenets and subsequent development of his methodological corpus. The resultant model, it is hoped, will be "Weberian;" but it does not claim the distinction of somehow being a representation or reconstruction of Weber's own thought. Despite the admitted confusions and contradictions of his writings, efforts to systematize Weber's methodology may bear productive results that extend beyond mere historical interest.

PART I

THE HISTORICAL DIMENSION OF WEBER'S METHODOLOGY

CHAPTER 1

EARLY RESEARCH EFFORTS

Weber's thought, ranging from highly abstract methodological speculations to concrete requirements for social science research, can be seen as comprising four fundamental purposes: (1) outlining the requirements for establishing of a basis of certainty for knowledge of the social world; (2) developing an elaborate array of constructs that allow for comparison of social phenomena; (3) analyzing empirical and historical reality utilizing these constructs; and (4) developing a rational perspective enabling the researcher to assess the forms of social action in terms of their meanings, including the explication of the causes of these meanings (cf. Freund, 1968:135).

The methodological problems--and the perceived solutions to these problems--were largely a result of several influential sources existing within Weber's historical milieu. These included issues that surfaced as a result of Weber's little-known research efforts, two "crises" of social science methodology that occurred during this period--termed the "Methodenstreit" and the "Werturteilstreit"--and the neo-Kantian perspective Weber adopted in an effort to resolve the methodological problems that confronted the social sciences.

Weber's initial efforts were largely historically- or empirically-based research treatises. Thus, they were distinct from his more substantive works, written at a later date. These studies, which may be dated from 1889 until his mental collapse in 1897, won Weber wide acclaim among his contemporaries as an innovative researcher (cf. Saloman, 1934; Marianne Weber, 1975; Kaesler, 1979). Ironically, they have remained largely unknown in both the German or the English-speaking worlds. Oberschall (1965:141) has noted that:

> Max Weber's efforts to establish an enduring tradi-
> tion of empirical social research have so far never
> been documented. One reason is that they ended in
> failure, whereas his historical works were such ob-
> vious successes.

An additional reason for this current lack of recognition of Weber's early empirical works is that they often remained unfinished. They remained either as outlines for further development, or as suggestions for and critiques of other researchers. Speculation regarding Weber's inability to complete many of his empirical projects have included accounts of Weber's "psychological problems"

(Lazarsfeld and Oberschall, 1965); Heckmann's (1979:50) assertion that Weber's empirical work was "...overloaded with too great a number of research problems and questions;" and Bendix's (1971:40) comment that the combination of the internal struggles of the German Sociological Association (that Weber had helped to found, in the hope of furthering the development of objective research), in combination with the onset of World War I, interrupted much of the empirical research being conducted in Germany at the time. [1]

While these comments are indicative of the attention accorded to the reasons for the "failures" of Weber's research programs, other efforts have been directed toward an explication of the methodological elements that Weber began to develop during this period. Bruun (1972), for example, has attempted to demonstrate that Weber's concern for value freedom was reflected in his earliest empirical studies of Polish workers in East Prussia. Henrich (1952) has argued that Weber's entire methodological corpus constituted a unified argument, implying that the empirical studies Weber undertook were also fully developed along the methodological lines he propounded.

---

[1] Bendix (1971:42) has also remarked that, through the vehicle of the German Sociological Association, Weber "...suggested team projects on the press, voluntary associations, and the relationship of technology and culture. He did manage to gather funds for the press study, but the project collapsed when he resigned from the directorship after a lawsuit against a journalist. Other team projects never materialized since his colleagues were unwilling to abandon their accustomed work style."

There is much evidence, additionally, which suggests that these empirical studies confronted Weber with concrete problems that led him to develop more abstract methodological formulations; e.g., the problem of discovering historical equivalents (cf. Tenbruck, 1959). Thus, these studies often contain far more value than their actual content suggests with only a cursory examination. The problems inherent in the studies occupied Weber throughout his career, and they represent the inception of his attempts to resolve empirical problems that arose as a direct result of these investigations. Thus, Weber's subsequent methodological treatises were informed by the considerations generated by his early historical and empirical work.

Much confusion exists regarding the status of Weber's works as comprising a fully-developed methodology for sociological investigation. While Henrich (1952) has argued that the theme of Weber's work never changed, Mommsen (1974) and Winckelmann (in Graber, 1981) have contended that Weber's notion of an "interpretive sociology," with its attendant concepts, was not in evidence until at least 1913.[2] There is a general consensus that Weber did not

---

[2] The work that is often given as a mark of Weber's transition from a historical to a sociological methodologist was published in 1913. It has been translated into English by Edith Graber with the title: "Some Categories of Interpretive Sociology" (1913). Although The Protestant Ethic is often thought to mark Weber's first "sociological" treatise, he remarked in a letter to Rickert (April 2, 1909), that

complete a methodological system; nor did he even identify himself as a methodologist until relatively late in his career (cf. Tenbruck, 1959). Eliaeson (1977:40) has asserted that: "Weber's methodology is never fulfilled in the sense that it has not been presented by Weber as a coherent whole. Rather, it is polemical and context-bound." Bruun (1972:10) has remarked that "...it seems reasonable to conclude that there are not sufficient grounds to suppose that Weber, in writing [his] methodological articles...aimed at constructing a systematic sociology." However, it is in Weber's dissertation, Habilitationschrift,[3] and early empirical investigations that the sense is conveyed that the questions arising as a result of these studies would ultimately lead Weber to begin the development of a sociological methodology.

DISSERTATION AND HABILITATIONSCHRIFT

Weber's dissertation was completed in 1889, entitled: ["On the History of Trading Associations in the Middle Ages" D]. Roth (1978:x) has summarized this early effort by Weber:

> Based largely on Italian sources, it dealt with various forms of limited and unlimited partnership

---

this work was not a sociological exercise, but an "essay in cultural history."

[3] In Germany, a "Habilitation" is the degree beyond the doctorate allowing successful candidates to apply for academic positions.

that emerged with the revival of maritime and inland trade and craft production.

The dissertation was also a combined study of legal and economic history, and considered the processes of bureaucratization and democratization. Weber (1889:44) outlined the basic conditions leading to the emergence of incipient capitalism, which included the separation of the economic sphere from the locus of the family, and the impact of Germanic law on the development of the capitalistic enterprise (Firma). The central argument presented in the dissertation was that individualistic Roman law had failed to keep pace with the developments associated with the emerging requirements of modern capitalism (cf. Kaesler, 1979:31). The direction of his work was to change during the years immediately following the completion of the dissertation, as Weber failed to obtain, in his estimation, significant evidence for the thesis of his dissertation (Roth, 1978:xxxiv). Nevertheless, he demonstrated high competence in the areas of jurisprudence and history, and Weber incorporated many of these findings in his later works.[4]

This initial investigation provided the groundwork for Weber's Habilitationsschrift (published in 1891), entitled [Roman Agrarian History and Its Meaning for State and Private Law. F] The central themes of the

---

[4] See, e.g., "The Impact of Trade on the Development of Patrimonialism" (in Weber, 1978a:1092-1097).

Habilitationsschrift followed those of the dissertation, in its study of the conditions for the development of capitalism. However, there was an additional emphasis on the development of capitalism in the province of Roman agriculture. Weber (1891:129) remarked that because of the Roman partitioning of land through occupation and improved cultivation, there was an unprecedented buildup of capital:

> [...these unrestrained occurrences proved beneficial not to the peasant farmer, but solely to the business magistrates... Their accomplishment was the realization of unbridled capitalism in the agricultural sphere...and this serves as a model not far removed from the above-mentioned infringements and encroachments, both quantitatively and qualitatively, of the landlord of the late middle ages. G]

Additionally, Weber's observations regarding the consequences of these developments for various classes of individuals (e.g., slaves and serfs), signaled Weber's early shift from a purely historical account of legal and economic forces (as expressed in his dissertation), toward a focus more sociological in nature (Heuss, 1965). Also, Weber initiated the development of his ideal-type concepts of patrimonialism and the domination of charismatic leaders, although his later emphasis on the separation of the sphere of values from that of science remained conspicuously absent (Roth, 1978:xli-xliii).

Kaesler (1979:33-34) has asserted that three aspects of Weber's thought began their development at this point: (1) the comparative approach, in his treatment of divergent legal systems; (2) the possibility for a "disharmonious development" between institutions--in this case, between legal and economic institutions; and (3) the emerging patterns of social differentiation, which indicated the possibility for the development of different types of legal and economic systems. Thus, against the "emanatism" that was prevalent during the time of his writing, Weber envisioned an entirely different type of social dynamic, in which the concrete actions of individuals and associations became the appropriate locus of interest for social scientists. Weber (1891:2) remarked that ["...the existence of a connection between two historical appearances becomes evident not in the abstract, but can only be established with a systematic consideration of how the concrete appearances of this connection have occurred." H] Additionally, Weber's initial consideration of his methodological concept of the ideal type can be seen at this point. Although he termed them "Idealbildern" (ideal concepts), even at this stage of his writing Weber appeared to be conscious of both their limitations and utility:

> [If one isolates the tendencies of any development, it must always be accompanied by the reservation that these are only tendencies...that may never be realized in their pure forms. Nevertheless one can, I believe, formulate these tendencies in terms of ideal concepts...(Weber, 1891:266) I]

Weber's use of value-loaded terms to describe cultural change--e.g., the "deterioration" (Untergang) of cultures;

and their "process of recovery" (Gesundungsprozess), as well as his overt sympathy for the social and material conditions of slaves--indicates that his position vis-a-vis value freedom was not yet in evidence (cf. Kaesler, 1979:41). Although Weber later acknowledged several additional errors in this work, he remained faithful to many of the central tenets developed at this point over the remainder of his career. These concerns are elaborated in Weber's (1896) essay: "The Social Grounds for the Decline of Ancient Culture," and further explicated in a 1908 treatise entitled "Agrarian Conditions in Antiquity."[5] Heuss (1965:538) has remarked that: ["The topic of 'agrarian history' (in these later essays) is...far exceeded; their treatment extends to an outline of social and economic history in the ancient world" J].

STUDIES WITH THE VEREIN FUER SOZIALPOLITIK

It was for his efforts during this period that Weber won acclaim as an empirical researcher. Weber was a member of the Verein fuer Sozialpolitik (founded in 1872), which became the central organization for the development of survey research during the period of 1880-1900 in Germany. The first Verein-sponsored research in which Weber took an active role was an inquiry into the existence of rural

---

[5] By the time of his 1896 essay, Weber substituted the term "Idealschema" (ideal scheme or pattern) for the earlier "Idealbildern."

laborers in the German provinces. Three thousand questionnaires were distributed, and members of the Verein then independently undertook analyses of the data, which were classified by geographic region. Weber undertook the analysis of the data from Eastern Prussia.

In this section of the study, defined geographically as the district of Prussia east of the Elbe River, the situation was unique in several respects, encompassing a wide spectrum of social differentiation. Primarily, Weber was interested in the transition from the traditional contractual form of labor to wage labor, which was common in the more industrialized western provinces.[6] These conditions provided Weber with the opportunity to develop new methodological techniques, and his subsequent innovations were destined to have a significant influence on his later methodological thought. The rural workers, traditionally, had been German peasants who were tied by a form of social relation--termed "Gutherrschaft"--to a political class of rural landholders (the Junkers) in a manner that contained several characteristics similar to those of feudalism. For example, workers were "bound" to their owners by tradition, and were permitted a small parcel of land to farm for their own profit. Weber found, however, that this system was breaking down, and that the German workers were being

---

[6] Weber's initial account of these conditions is contained in a 1892 essay: "The Relations of Agricultural Workers in Eastern Germany."

replaced by Polish and Russian workers. These foreign workers were willing to work for a wage; and the extent to which this occurred indicated the transition, Weber posited, from a feudalistic system to that of "fully-developed capitalism" (Hochkapitalismus).[7]

Weber presented an extensive (890 page) report to the Verein in 1892-1893. However, what was most important for his later methodological development, was Weber's position with respect to values and to concrete methods of social investigation. In an early report of his findings, Weber (1893b) stressed the political implications of the results, rather than adhering to an objective presentation. Weber asserted that the in-migration of workers--primarily from Poland--accompanied by the exodus of German workers, was producing a situation that threatened the national boundary to the east. Weber argued that the Junkers were failing in their role as a leading economic class in Germany by allowing Germany to be thus "weakened" on one of its borders. Further, having joined the study after the design of the questionnaire was completed, Weber offered several suggestions for its subsequent improvement. Foremost among these was the exaggerated focus of the Verein on the material conditions of the workers, at the expense of denying their "subjective states," which Weber believed was

---

[7] For an account of the conditions existing in this region prior to the study of the Verein, see Bendix (1960:37-43).

equally important:

> ...the question is not how high the income of the
> workers really is, but whether as a result of (the
> level of wages) an orderly economy is possible for
> the workers, whether he and his employer are satis-
> fied according to their own subjective evaluation,
> or why they are not, what direction their wishes and
> aspirations are taking, for future development will
> depend on these factors (Weber, 1892:67).

EMERGING METHODOLOGICAL CONCERNS

Thus, Weber's emerging concern with the interrelationship of cultural values and the economic motives of individuals becomes evident in his works from this point (cf. Bendix, 1960:52). In a project designed to correct what Weber viewed as a neglect of these factors, he joined with the Evangelical-Social Congress to conduct a new study. The questionnaire, designed in large part by Weber, was "shorter, divided into more meaningful units, and the questions were more precise" (Lazarsfeld and Oberschall, 1965:186). Moreover, the questionnaires of the earlier Verein study were sent to employers. Weber, rejecting the validity of the employers' claims to assess accurately the conditions of the workers, instead distributed the new questionnaires to lay ministers in the same area. The ministers, Weber reasoned, were closer to the conditions of the workers, and were capable of apprehending their circumstances with more accuracy.

Two aspects of Weber's methodological thought began their development from this point. First, Weber demonstrated a preoccupation with the improvement of existing empirical techniques. He was the sole researcher involved in the project to compare his results with those of earlier studies, in an effort to achieve a more diachronic analysis (Heckmann, 1979:52). The improvement of techniques of data gathering, unfortunately, was not reflected in his ability to interpret the data. For example, Weber (1893a:540) remarked that:

["....There can be no doubt that this material remains a puzzle: We have not yet discovered a method of evaluating it. Anyone who has not joined in such an undertaking cannot conceive of the magnitude of such an effort. The unique freshness of the accounts in their raw form will, for the most part, be lost." K]

Even in a report published six years later, Weber remained at a loss to interpret these data (Lazarsfeld and Oberschall, 1965:187). His methodological efforts during the latter part of his career represent an attempt to overcome this obstacle. Nevertheless, these research efforts--the first of six times that he was involved in empirical research--won Weber national prominence as a leading methodologist (Oberschall, 1965; Lazarsfeld and Oberschall, 1965; Salomon, 1934; Bendix and Roth, 1971). Secondly, Weber's concern with the status of economic motives and national policy assumed paramount importance. This did not, however, entail any notion of developing a eudaemonistic national economic policy based on a "science of economics." For example, Weber remarked in 1894 that:

> Insofar as it is in our power, we wish to arrange external conditions not with a view toward people's well-being, but in such a way as to preserve...those physical and spiritual qualities that we would like to maintain for the nation (Weber, in Marianne Weber (1975:137).

The paradoxical effect of this position was that it led Weber, in later polemical accounts, to argue for the value-freedom of the sciences.

Finally, it was in his Antrittsrede, or introductory speech, read on the occasion of his appointment to an academic position in Freiburg in 1895, that Weber demonstrated a knowledge of the methodological problems with which he would later be concerned (cf. Bruun, 1972:59).[8] In the Antrittsrede, Weber related the results of his earlier studies in the Verein, but again substituted a practical discussion of the results for the theoretical conclusions that had been expected (Bruun, 1972:54). Instead, Weber repeated earlier themes, directly linking the simultaneous weakening of the eastern border of Prussia through the rapid influx of foreign workers and the decline of the Junkers, to a discussion of the criteria that must be established in the formation of economic policy. This discussion, then, became Weber's foil for engaging in an initial excursus regarding

---

[8] Der Nationalstaat und die Volkswirtschaftspolitik: Akademische Antrittsrede.

the relationship of values to science.

Weber's central premise was that values cannot be established within the science of economics, but rather must be generated externally. His criticism was thus tacitly directed against those who advocated a form of economics oriented toward a vague goal of establishing the greatest material good for all the members of the society.[9] Weber argued that this "external" value, moreover, is always one that is determined by national interests. Any effort to deny this, he suggested, only evaded the "burden of decision" that was necessarily placed on the individuals responsible for the determination of national economic policy.

Tenbruck (1959) has argued that this amounted to a fundamental "ignorance" of any true establishment of a methodological position vis-a-vis values in science, while others have claimed that this marks Weber's earliest statements regarding the intrusion of values into scientific method (Mommsen, 1959). Bruun (1972), while taking the latter position, has further suggested that Weber's consideration of the sphere of values may be divided into three categories of fundamentally distinct statements. The first two categories he terms "asymmetrical;" the third "symmetrical." Bruun's thesis is that Weber first argued, although not exclusively, that the sphere of science must be

---

[9] This policy was termed the "Volkswohlstand."

kept separate from the sphere of values, but not the reverse. Thus, e.g., the economic sphere is not constrained to establish any "scientific" basis for economic values, but science may provide the means for the achievement of cultural or national goals. The Antrittsrede illustrates the culmination of this position.

The second category of statements represents the obverse argument: that the sphere of values must be kept free from the sphere of science. Finally, the "symmetrical" assertion by Weber was that both the spheres of science and values must be closed to one another, and that the intrusion of either into the sphere of the other violates the potential of both. The central themes of these writings suggest that, during the early phase of Weber's career, he was able only to establish the "asymmetrical" conclusion that "external" (i.e., religious, political, etc.) values must be kept free from scientific method.

Thus, it is clear that the largely unknown works by Weber incorporate aspects that were to be developed in his more widely-acclaimed writings. His empirical work, while often tentative and incomplete, gave rise to methodological and substantive issues that have defined much of the problematic not only for Weber's contemporaries, but for modern sociologists. They provide evidence of Weber's early attempts to construct ideal types, the construction of empirical typologies, the concern with the interactions of subjective states of individuals with their material conditions, and his preoccupation with the relationship of science to values. Taken together, these writings comprise valuable insights not only into the methodological questions that confronted Weber, but also the lines along which he attempted to forge the answers.

CHAPTER II

THE METHODENSTREIT AND THE WERTURTEILSTREIT

During this early period, many of Weber's concrete empirical concerns gave rise to larger problems that would cause him to become more deeply involved in methodological issues. Weber's heightened commitment to the resolution of purely methodological problems arose during a period in which a "crisis of method" (the Methodenstreit) was beginning to dominate intellectual circles in Germany. Additionally, Weber gradually became enmeshed in the debate over the place of "values" in the social sciences. Largely as a result of Weber's polemics against Gustav von Schmoller and members of the "Historical School," the "Werturteilstreit" ("crises of values") emerged in the German social sciences, and the result was a questioning of the entire foundation of the social sciences.

It was within this historical context that much of Weber's subsequent thought developed; and, as Burger (1976:10) has suggested: "There is little hope for a proper understanding of Weber without an adequate conception of the problem situation as he perceived it." Weber utilized selected elements of the writing of several German thinkers, who were also responding to the concerns of the Methodenstreit, with the assumption that the background of the writers was sufficiently known to his audience to leave it untreated in any systematic or comprehensive manner. This has led to several problems regarding the origins of the context of Weber's methodological thought. Thus, an overview of this context, and the major intellectual responsible for significantly influencing the content of Weber's position, is necessary in order to understand more fully Weber's methodological intent.

THE METHODENSTREIT

In the mid-19th century, Hegelian philosophy reached its nadir, largely as a result of the failure of the revolution in 1848 (Kamenka, 1983), and a general sense of despair began to emerge in German thought regarding the status of philosophy. This, in turn, ultimately led to doubts surrounding the certainty of the sciences themselves (Willey, 1978:24). As Oakes (1982:595) has remarked:

> The critique of Hegelian idealism which had appeared in Berlin in the 1830's and 1840's was generalized to form a critique of the entire project of metaphysics. Doubts about the possibility of metaphysics led to more comprehensive suspicions about the possibility of philosophy in general. This skepticism generated doubts about the legitimacy of the sociocultural sciences...(and) the malaise of Weber's immediate predecessors was an expression of this predicament. What had begun as an apparently provincial or even local dispute--the controversies which arose in Berlin over Hegel's work in the years immediately following his death--reached the proportions of a general crisis of intellectuality.

In the case of the social sciences, this crisis was also precipitated by a naive form of scientism, in which the methods that engendered the unprecedented progress experienced by the natural sciences were adopted uncritically as a model for all the sciences. Thus, the methods of physics, chemistry, and particularly physiology became paradigmatic for what were termed, at the time, the "historical" sciences (Willey, 1978). The extremes to which this practice was extended were exhibited by the widely-accepted contention by Moleshott (in Randall, 1965:376), who accounted for mental activity by declaring that the brain "secretes thoughts in the same manner in which the liver secretes bile;" and the related claim that "...matter, with its primary properties and their relations as revealed by science, are the ultimate realities, and that human bodies are mechanisms, though occasionally controlled...by minds" (Dampier, 1948:289).

These two events, the decline of Hegelianism and the rise of scientific positivism, ultimately gave rise to the general controversies of the Methodenstreit, which crystallized around two general areas of debate (cf. Oakes, 1975: 17-20): (1) whether or not the sociocultural disciplines could be considered nomological sciences--if not, they appeared to be doomed to a relativism that was inconsistent with the basic canons of science; (2) the possibility that the subject matter of these disciplines might be fundamentally different from that of the natural sciences--i.e., although the methods of the natural sciences had been immensely productive during this era, could they be utilized with the same degree of success in the emerging social sciences?

NEO-KANTIANISM

The increasing controversy engendered by this debate gave rise to several conflicting positions. However, increasing credence in German philosophical and scientific circles during the period was accorded the position of thinkers such as Helmholz and Liebig (cf. Willey, 1978:25-26). These authors argued that the resolution of the debate could only occur through a return, in some fashion, to Kantian principles.

Thus, the neo-Kantian revival--characterized by the shibboleth, "Back to Kant"--began as a positive response to the questions posed during this period of German intellectual history, and ultimately formed much of the basis for Weber's own methodological thought (cf. Parsons, 1965:172; Giddens, 1978:138). Although the works of the neo-Kantians reflected several differences, four basic Kantian assumptions distinguished them from other attempts[1] to resolve the Methodenstreit: (1) they began with the transcendental approach (as opposed to empirical and

---

[1] For example, organic positivism (cf. Martindale, 1959).

psychological approaches) in their inquiries--i.e., they sought the conditions that exist "prior" to knowledge; (2) they emphasized the importance of the concept for understanding of the world (as opposed, e.g., to intuitionism and reliance on an "essence"), and thus the indispensability of rationality; (3) they operated on the idealist assumption that direct knowledge of any object cannot be apprehended. Rather, the object represents the primacy of practical reason over pure reason; (4) while emphasizing the subjectivity of consciousness, they attempted, in conjunction with their focus on the concept of value, to establish the objectivity of the social sciences.

The neo-Kantians, then, assigned to the notion of values not only an ontological, but also an axiological status. It was along these general lines that Weber formed his methodological perspective, in his adopting the thinking of--and often critical reaction to--those who developed these tenets. Although there were several neo-Kantian groups, two predominant schools emerged in Germany at the time Weber began his methodological investigations: the Marburg School, and the Southwestern, or Baden group.

The Marburg School was the first to reassert the rationality of the human mind as a response to the positivistic extremism that engendered the Methodenstreit (Iggers, 1968). However, this school exerted only an indirect influence on Weber's thought, as its leaders,

Hermann Cohen and Paul Natorp, emphasized the reliance of reason not on the gathering of sense data, but on the assumption that consciousness alone is "real" (Iggers, 1968:144-145). This gradually led to a renewed concern with Kantian ethics and the implications for the establishment of a society based on the Categorical Imperative (Willey, 1978:132).

As the Marburg School developed further, it began to associate a universalistic conception of ethics with the goals of science (Willey, 1978:102-105), and to deny the importance of irrationality as one factor of human behavior that is amenable to scientific investigation (cf. Iggers, 1968:144-145). Clearly, these tenets were of the sort that Weber's philosophy of science was reacting against, and this reaction finds its fullest expression in his "Critique of Stammler" (Weber, 1907 in 1978a:325-333).

In opposition to the Marburg School, the Baden group exerted a significant positive influence on Weber's methodological thought. Questions of "ethics" or "values" became important for this school in a more theoretical sense, rather than as objective entities that required concrete application. Its leaders, Windelband and Rickert, were to establish positions vis-a-vis the Methodenstreit that formed, in large part, the basis for Weber's methodology (Burger, 1976; Oakes, 1980; Marianne Weber, 1975). The Baden School was founded on the assumption that all societies share, according to Willey (1978:132): "the order of rational moral precepts, a historical process infused with the ideal purposes of man, and a cultural life measured by enduring, universal standards of value." Thus, whereas the Marburger, Stammler, sought the universal nature of law and a mode for its practical application, the Baden neo-Kantians were concerned with the universal nature of values, and its significance for the analysis of individual conduct (cf. Willey, 1978). Thus, they increasingly turned their attention toward the importance of this assumption for social science methodology.

Windelband and the Baden School. Based on this discussion of values, Windelband responded to the issues posed during the Methodenstreit by reformulating the division between the natural and the social sciences.[2] The goals of the various sciences, Windelband argued, should be used to mark the distinction between the methods of the sciences, as well as their subject matter. Thus, in his famous "Rectorial Address," Windelband (1890:178) posited that:

> From the perspective of the natural scientist, the single datum is scientifically useful only to the

---

[2] Weber expressed his indebtedness to Windelband's thought at several junctures--see, e.g., his reference to Windelband in the discussion of verification in the essay, "The Meaning of Ethical Neutrality" (Weber, 1917 in Weber, 1949:41).

extent that the scientist believes he is justified
in representing the datum as a type, a special case
of a general concept.

From this, Windelband established the fundamental
distinction between "idiographic" and "nomothetic" sciences.
"Idiographic" refers to the description of the separate,
distinct, or individual--"sciences of the event"
(Windelband, 1980:175). "Nomothetic," in contrast, refers
to the aim of the natural sciences, which is to discover
"laws" that "invariably remain constant" (Windelband,
1980:175). Both nomothetic and idiographic sciences are
empirical, and both may initiate their investigation of a
problem utilizing either a generalizing or an
individualizing approach.

However, the ultimate task of the natural scientist is
fundamentally different from that of the historian. If, for
example, he or she merely isolated the relevant facts and
described them accurately, the natural scientist's
investigation would be incomplete: The facts obtained are
merely individual instances of more general laws or
principles. Conversely, for the historian to conclude that
"laws" can be somehow inferred from a collection of
historical facts, invites the possibility for the emergence
of historical determinism. Thus, for the purposes of the
historian, laws possess no utility:

General laws do not establish an ultimate state from
which the specific conditions of the causal chain
could ultimately be derived. It follows that all

subsumption under general laws is useless in the analysis of the ultimate causes or grounds of the single, temporarily given phenomena (Windelband, 1980:184).

Windelband succeeded in arguing for the abandonment of the distinction established by Dilthey between the "Naturwissenschaften" (natural sciences) and the "Geisteswissenschaften" ("mental" or "spiritual" sciences), and establishing the grounds for a distinction between natural science and history. However, Windelband largely ignored the unique problems presented by the emerging social sciences. These problems would be addressed more fully by his successor in the Baden School, Heinrich Rickert, and his proposed solutions ultimately adopted and reformulated by Weber (cf. Burger, 1976; Willey, 1978; Marianne Weber, 1975; Henrich, 1952).

Rickert and the Baden School. Rickert, like Windelband, asserted that different sciences could be distinguished by their utilization of diverging methods. However, several fundamental differences existed between these two thinkers. The most significant of these lay in the assertion by Rickert that Windelband did not realize that the division between "history" and "science" failed to establish distinctions that should be made explicit in the sciences themselves. Additionally, Rickert contended that the notion of "intuitive contemplation" (Anschaulichkeit), which Windelband contended could be used to grasp social reality, must be supplanted by a system of rational concepts.

Rickert's explication of these positions laid the foundation for Weber's methodological thought, to an extent that has only recently begun to receive adequate attention by sociologists (Burger, 1976; Willey, 1978). Rickert's exposition began by asserting that the social scientist does not begin an investigation through an evaluation (Wertung) of a problem; rather, he centers attention on a given "cultural object" (Kulturobject) that is "related through value" (Wertbezogene) by members of a society. Thus, against Dilthey, social existence cannot be understood by the direct apprehension of historical minds.

Rickert posited, instead, that the products of culture (Kulturgueter) themselves are understood through a process of relating them to concepts that are constructed according to the understanding that the scientist has of the phenomena, rather than relying on the assumption that they can be grasped through any immediate understanding that is not mediated by concepts. Thus, Rickert employed the concept "Kulturwissenschaft" ("cultural science"), as opposed to both Dilthey's distinction between "Geisteswissenschaften" and "Naturwissenschaften," and Windelband's separation of the nomothetic and idiographic modes of investigation. Thus, Rickert placed the cultural sciences much closer to the natural sciences in his formulation than to the methods or goals of the historical researcher (cf. Martindale, 1959:65; Burger, 1976:24).

However, two interrelated problems confronted Rickert at this juncture of his argument. First, if values are merely products of random, individual will, then the same sort of relativism that Rickert was attempting to overcome would resurface in the social sciences. Secondly, the reliance on the construction of concepts constituted a rejection of the "copy theory" of knowledge. Thus, the selection of the values that are directly relevant to the formation of a concept becomes of vital importance to the scientific enterprise as a whole.

In an effort to place these cultural sciences on an objective footing equal to that of the natural sciences, Rickert was first required (1926:95) to posit the existence of universal, transcendental values:

> [The fact that cultural values are universal is what keeps concept formation in the historical sciences from being subject to arbitrary caprice, yielding a foundation for the objectivity of these concepts. What is historically essential must be significant not for just this or that person, but for everyone.]

These values may be expressed in various manners in each culture. It would be a serious methodological error to assume that universal values are directly amenable to empirical investigation. For example, the notion of "progress," although it may be a universally held value, is a phenomenon that can only be studied in terms of developments that are unique in a given culture. To extend beyond this limit, and assume a single, empirically verifiable concept of "progress" in all societies, is a fundamental misconception of the boundaries of science. Thus, the question of the "progress" of societies as a whole could be addressed in the realm of the philosophy of history, but not in the bounds of any science that hopes to retain its claim to objectivity (Rickert, 1921:109-110). A social scientist may possess the ability to identify individual expressions of development in a society; however, the investigation of epiphenomena such as "progress" or "efficiency" (conceived apart from the meanings of acting individuals), always lies outside his sphere of competence. This has led Iggers (1968:157) to conclude that Rickert agreed with Kant that the "norms of ethics are universally valid and timeless...but these norms, central to which is the categorical imperative, are purely formal."

The world of empirical values, which forms the appropriate locus of concern for the social scientist, is the expression of these ultimate values. However, the number of empirical values, Rickert asserted, could approach infinity, both intensively and extensively, and comprehension of their totality is impossible:

> One need only make an attempt to "describe" reality exactly "as it is," i.e., to achieve a conceptual representation of it faithfully in all its details, to realize very soon how futile such an undertaking is. Empirical reality proves to be an immeasureable manifold which seems to become greater and greater

the more deeply we delve into it and begin to analyze it... For even the "smallest" part contains more than any mortal man has the power to describe. Indeed, the part of reality that man can include in his concepts, and thus in his knowledge, is almost infinitesimally small when compared to what he must disregard (Rickert, 1962:32).[3]

The principle for the isolation of the _correct_ values for the conceptualization of phenomena became essential, as no social phenomena could be studied in its multifaceted totality, nor can it be reduced to an "essence" through some process of intuition.

Following Kant, Rickert categorically rejected the possibility for the establishment of a eudaemonistic value theory (Willey, 1978:23). Rather, the selection of the relevant values must be in accordance with two basic principles. The first calls for a delineation of those aspects that are common to many phenomena. It thus involves the inclusion of only the most "essential" elements, while neglecting individual differences. This is the principle of selection for the construction of concepts that the sciences--both natural and social--follow. The second principle of selection, however, involves the isolation of those unique features of a congeries of interrelated events that are distinctive, in some specifiable manner, from all

---

[3] Compare this statement by Rickert to Weber's assertion five years later: "All the analysis of infinite reality which the finite human mind can conduct rests on the tacit assumption that only a finite portion of this reality con- stitutes the object of scientific investigation... (Weber, 1904 in Weber, 1949:72).

other events. This is the method in which historical events
(e.g., the factors leading to the decline of Rome) are
explicated.

Following Windelband, Rickert argued that both the
natural science and historical principles of concept
formation involve abstraction through reference to the
empirical. This extension and revision of Windelband's
thought provided Weber, in turn, with the methodological
justification for his ideal types, as well as for several
empirical research efforts in which he later became
involved.

Weber's neo-Kantian Response to the Methodenstreit

Weber's stated concern with the possible outcome and
response to the Methodenstreit spanned the latter half of
his career, and closely followed the arguments of Windelband
and Rickert (Iggers, 1968; Burger, 1976). These issues were,
however, addressed in rudimentary form even at the time of
his initial empirical works, beginning in 1893 (Kaesler,
1979:41). Stated broadly, Weber outlined two interrelated
positions in response to the Methodenstreit. First, he
asserted that the social sciences, unlike the natural
sciences, set as their goal for research a form of
explanation of social conduct in which, ultimately,
nomological laws play no part (Weber, 1949:89; cf. Oakes,
1975:36).

Thus, as Weber (1924b:113) stated, the social sciences are sciences of concrete reality, which employ abstract concepts as a _means_, and may even treat these as being "law-like." In reality, they are only general expressions that refer to the "rules governing rational conduct" (Weber, 1904 in Weber, 1949:74). These abstractions exist only as approximations that refer to the "selection and unification of those properties which are regarded (by the social scientist) as characteristic" (Weber, 1922 in Weber, 1975b:57). Thus, whereas the natural scientist wishes to increase the _extension_ of his concepts, this is not the ultimate objective of the social scientist.

Secondly, and as a result of this, the distinction between the natural and social sciences is not based on an ontological disparity between them; rather, the primary difference is axiological--i.e., the theoretical _interest_ of the social sciences diverges from the natural sciences, in that social action is "subjectively meaningful" (Weber, 1903 in 1975b:102-104). This "meaningfulness," according to Weber (1922 in Weber, 1978a:4), may be separated into two categories: (1) either the actual existing meaning in the concrete case to a given actor, or to an "average" meaning that may be attributed to an existing group of actors; or (2) a theoretically conceived _pure_ _type_ (Reintyp), that is attributed to the behavior of hypothetical actors engaged in a specified form of action. Weber added the qualification, at this juncture, that these meanings are not, in any sense, objectively "correct." In this manner, he wished to differentiate his position from that of Simmel, whom Weber accused of confounding subjective and objective meanings (Weber, 1975a:152), as well as from the "intuitionists" who argued that meanings, correctly apprehended, are objectively valid (Weber, 1903 in 1975b: 152). The social sciences require, as a result, a method of interpretive understanding (Verstehen), which is of a different type from the methods of the natural sciences, and yet rejects the possibility for achieving a "total" understanding as posited by the intuitionists.

Thus, much of Weber's methodological thought was informed by the writings of Rickert, Windelband, and the Baden School of neo-Kantianism, as Weber freely acknowledged (Weber, 1924b:4, 15n., 76n., 116n., 237n., 343n.; 1917 in 1949:21-22; 1903 in 1975b:211n). Willey (1978:163), for example, has asserted that Weber's ideal types are unquestionably the progeny of Rickert's "theoretical relation to values." It has also been well established that Weber engaged in several critiques and elaborations of the neo-Kantian position (Iggers, 1968; Freund, 1968; Marianne Weber, 1975; Goddard, 1973).

What is most important for those attempting to grasp Weber's intent, then, is to follow the directions that his attempted revision of these central theses took, and to discern the ways these led him either to a promising genesis of social science methodology; or conversely, to an untenable or ambiguous position. With respect to this latter point, Burger (1976:30-31), e.g., has stated that Rickert's account of how concepts are to be constructed in the social sciences was faulty: The "relevant elements," once chosen for the formation of a concept, do not share equal amounts of influence--as was supposed by Rickert--but exhibit them only in varying degrees. The failure to recognize this, it may be argued, also led Weber to overly simplistic conclusions in his development of ideal types.

THE WERTURTEILSTREIT

Weber began his own methodological excursus by attempting to resolve the issues of the Methodenstreit (Oakes, 1975). Closely related to the Methodenstreit, another crisis surfaced during the two decades prior to the onset of World War I. This controversy--termed the Werturteilstreit-- embroiled social scientists in a debate regarding the status of values in scientific investigation.[4]

However, the Werturteilstreit was solely concerned with the status of values in the social sciences, and their relationship to practical activity. The focus of the

---

[4] Although their emphasis vis-a-vis the social sciences differed, the Methodenstreit and the Werturteilstreit have often been treated as part of one debate (see, e.g. Freund, 1968; Schneider, 1975).

Werturteilstreit was thus narrower than that of the Methodenstreit, and involved Weber in a debate with a number of social scientists with diametrically opposed positions regarding the role of the sciences. Many of Weber's polemic methodological writings were formulated in response to the concerns of the Werturteilstreit, including critiques of the concept of the "Volksgeist," developed by the economist Roscher (1903); Knies' emphasis on the "irrationality" of social life (1903); Stammler's confusion of the systematization of abstract concepts with natural law (1907); Marx's "historical determinism" (1904-1905; 1922); the historian Meyer's methodological distinction between "free will" and "determinism" (1906); and Schmoller's view of the relationship of values to social science method (1884; 1904; 1905).

The two sides of the controversy were formed largely as a result of an exchange between Gustav von Schmoller, an economist of the emerging "historical school;" and Carl Menger, a protagonist of the older, more established classical school of economics.[5] Schmoller, while acknowledging that certain observable regularities existed in the economic sphere, asserted that the attendant complex

---

[5] The debate began with Menger's attack on the school of thought headed by Schmoller, with a treatise entitled: "Investigation of the Methods of the Social Sciences; with Special Reference to Political Economy," written in 1883. Schmoller's equally stinging response, written in the same year, was entitled "Methodologie."

of social behavior obviated the possibility for any development of a system of laws in the science of economics. Rather, relatively precise concepts could be formulated only after an exhaustive historical analysis of the causes of economic behaviors, followed by a categorization of events into "meaningful" patterns (cf. Bruun, 1972:81-82). Further, Schmoller argued for the possibility of the establishment of an _active_ role for economics in directing the course of practical activities, stating that economists must not only understand the course of economic development, but to predict future events and recommend certain economic measures as societal ideals (Schmoller, 1920).

As the debate grew, Weber emerged as a leader of the "value free" position, and was very soon identified as a "radical left-wing" member of the Verein (Dahrendorf, 1968). A year earlier, Weber, together with his colleagues Jaffe and Sombart, as editors of the journal, _Archiv fuer Sozialwissenschaft und Politik_, published their intention to separate value-laden policy recommendations from social science:

> Inevitably, problems of social _policy_ will...find expression in this journal...alongside those of so-cial _science_. But we would not dream of pretending that such discussions can be described as "science," and we will see to it that they are not confused with it (Weber, et al., 1904).

The intent of the editors was clearly polemical, and it led Weber and the "value free" social scientists to form a separate association, the Deutsche Gesellschaft fuer Soziologie (German Sociological Association), whose specific purpose was the rejection of all "...concern with practical (ethical, religious, political, esthetic, etc.) goals of any kind" (Weber et al., 1911:8). This statement, as well as similar arguments by Weber, have produced widespread confusion regarding his intent. For example, one year after his death, Honigsheim (1921:35) wrote that:

> Of all the things Max Weber did, said, and wrote, nothing has been as much talked about, commented on, misunderstood, and laughed off as his doctrine of a value-free approach in sociology.

Despite his failure to convince others of the merits of his position, the Werturteilstreit was a highly significant factor in the development of Weber's methodology. Through a series of polemical works, beginning at the turn of the century and lasting until his death in 1920, Weber sought to clarify his position. Both Weber's methodological and substantive works during the last phase of his life reflect a concern with the special position of values in the social sciences.

Weber's purposes from this point reflected the attempt, largely neo-Kantian in its focus, to develop a form of sociology that could result in an objective analysis of social life. His methodological stance reflects a preoccupation with social values expressed in terms of individual meaningfulness, while retaining cognizance of both the values of the researcher and social science itself.

Thus, in response to the position established by the positivists, Weber insisted that social scientists maintain an advantage over their natural science counterparts: the meanings imparted by their subjects could be known. However, this required an intersubjective dimension in social science methodology. As a result, Weber began the development of an "interpretive" sociological methodology ("verstehende Soziologie") that would inform his later methodological writings and empirical works.

CHAPTER III

LATER STAGES IN THE DEVELOPMENT OF WEBER'S

METHODOLOGICAL THOUGHT

The period of 1908-1920 marked, in Weber's methodological works, a gradual shift from his polemical writings of the Werturteilstreit toward the development of a more positive methodological program. With the continuance of his empirical work, an emphasis on conceptual rigor and value-freedom began to emerge. In contrast with Weber's earlier studies and the pronouncements in his methodological writings (as exemplified by the Antrittsrede of 1895), his work of this period more clearly reflected concerns which remain evident in contemporary sociology.

It was in these later writings, then, that Weber arrived at a series of complex methodological formulations, and attempted to integrate them more fully (if not always more explicitly) into his substantive thought. There is also evidence suggesting that Weber refrained from further polemics only with some reluctance.[1] Thus, it is still possible to discover, during this stage of his writings, strident critiques of his opponents. However, these are

---

[1] See, e.g., Weber, 1913 in Weber, 1981:279.

found, for the most part, in scattered footnotes and passim references, rather than in the titles or the main arguments of several of the earlier works.

EMPIRICAL WORKS

Despite the antagonisms generated during the Werturteilstreit, Weber was once again drawn into Verein-sponsored empirical research in 1908. The proposed study was an effort to ascertain the effects on workers, as well as their modes of adaptation, to work in large-scale industries. Although his brother Alfred and others initiated the study, Weber quickly assumed leadership of the project. The study was then transformed from a descriptive account of occupational activities to a more theoretically-based investigation that included, once again, efforts to assess the "subjective life" of the workers:

> [This study attempts to establish: On one side, what effects the large-scale industry exerts over individual character, occupational fate and "lifes-tyle" external to the workplace; what physical and mental qualities it helps to develop, and how these qualities are manifested in the workers' daily lives; on the other side, how the present and future development of large-scale industry is influenced, through the ethnic, social, and cultural origins of the workers, and their traditions and standards of living (Weber, 1904:1) L].

In designing the study, Weber incorporated what were, at the time, two innovative procedures: the direct questioning of the workers themselves; and the adoption of the position that any policy relevance was not to be an immediate concern or motivating factor of the research. Thus, Weber's attempts to achieve an understanding of the subjective conditions of respondents transcended his concern for the inability of the working-classes to give meaningful answers,[2] and was indicative of his concern for value-freedom in social science research.

Weber's plan for the study was presented in a series of articles under the heading, ["On the Psychophysics of Industrial Work" (Weber, 1908c) M]. Additionally, a separate article, ["Methodological Introduction to the Investigation of the Verein fuer Sozialpolitik Regarding Selection and Adaptation (Occupational Choice and Occupational Fate) of the Workers in Self-Contained Large Industry" (Weber, 1908b) N], detailed procedures for compilation and analysis of the material.

Of overriding significance in these methodological essays was Weber's initial attempt to conceptualize a social science methodology that made explicit the relationship between theory, Verstehen, and empirical research (Lazarsfeld and Oberschall, 1965). Although Weber presented his argument in an often ambiguous and tentative manner (cf. Oberschall, 1965), these ideas represent, for the first time, Weber's consideration of the role of Verstehen within

---

[2] Lazarsfeld and Oberschall (1965) have commented that this was a central topic of social theorists and researchers, in an era when "working- or lower-class behavior" was associated with characteristics such as inferior race, intelligence, or morality.

an empirical context.[3] Weber's approach also included a fundamental consideration of instrumental rationality, and its shading off into other, less directly understandable forms of social behavior. His rationality-irrationality continuum in these writings is unique, as he also considered the possibility of a purely mechanistic, "psycho-physical" form of action similar to Taylorism.[4]

At one end of this spectrum, Weber included variables that focused on the rational actions of the workers: ["...the workers regulate their activities according to their calculations of "material" (i.e., "earnings") goals..." (Weber, 1908c in Weber, 1924a:132) 0]. The "behavior maxims" of these actions are, Weber asserted, "pragmatically interpretable." At the opposite end of this continuum, are "psycho-physical" variables, that are best understood in terms of their effects, and can be measured in the same way as a natural scientist might measure the energy of output by any organic material:

> [...the point that is interesting from the perspec-
> tive of causation, similar to the progress in meas-
> urement in biochemistry, to make a special case of a
> rule, introspective conceptual ability is not the
> "cause" (of the behavior); on the contrary, it is

---

[3] The term "empirical" is used here in its more contemporary association with quantitative research, rather than its broader meaning, which connotes reliance on experientially-derived facts (cf. Hospers, 1967).

[4] Weber was not influenced by Taylor, whose work was unknown in Germany at the time. However, Weber relied heavily upon the writings of Abbe, an early industrial psychologist in Germany (Oberschall, 1965).

for us of singularly secondary importance (Weber, 1908c in 1924a:133) P].

Thus, in order to obtain these types of data, the workers would not need to be queried directly, nor would this behavior require intersubjective understanding. Rather, reference to production curves and the like are sufficient to obtain the relevant information.

Between these two extremes, Weber posited the existence of a "gray zone" of the workers' subjective states of which the workers are cognizant, but do not realize causes changes in their productive output. Weber contended that this phenomena can be understood, but not as readily as "rational goal-oriented activity" or "psycho-physical" states. What must be accomplished, he posited, was an interpretive understanding of the motives of the workers.

Although Weber conceded, in characteristic fashion, that this discussion was not fully developed, he maintained that a consideration of the entire range of these variables was necessary for the successful completion of the study. Thus, he saw three interrelated processes as being essential for the construction of this form of research: (1) the explanation of existing, readily comprehensible data, including "psychophysical" data; (2) an interpretation of the means consciously employed by the workers to obtain ends consciously realized, and thus readily "calculable" by the researcher; and (3) two forms of understanding. The first requires the researcher to acquire the relevant knowledge regarding the societal conditions that serve as factors in shaping behavior; the second form of understanding requires the researcher to imaginatively reconstruct motives and feelings of which the subjects might not either be aware or be able to articulate. The conclusion that each type of variable was, ultimately, capable of empirical assessment was obvious to Weber; only the mode of their apprehension would vary. Oberschall (1965:118) has remarked that:

> Of course the method of measurement would differ: For example, (in the case of) rational motives of which the worker is conscious, he might be able to verbalize, whereas the unconscious motives or states of mind might have to be gotten out of him through projective devices.

Weber acknowledged, (1908c in 1924a:238) however, that each method remained imprecise in relation to the laboratory experiments of the natural sciences. Not even the "psycho-physical" material, obtained in a relatively straightforward fashion, was completely free from error.

With respect to the study of industrial workers, these propositions were revolutionary. Weber became cognizant that measurement of output would need to be obtained not only through an assessment of rational, but also what he termed "economically irrational" states of mind: [...the 'disposition' of the workers, and particularly their shifting relations with their employers...has often been reported, although without full proof" (Weber, 1908c in

1924a:155) Q].

Unfortunately, Weber's extensive efforts in designing the study failed to produce sufficient motivation for the workers to respond. Although attempts were made over a two-year period to collect the data, fewer than 10% of the questionnaires were returned. Several members of the Verein persisted in demonstrating their enthusiasm for even these "findings;" however, Weber was not equally moved (Weber, 1911a, in 1924b:424). The meager rate of return led him to suggest methods for analyzing an extensive body of data already collected by Adolph Levenstein. Weber maintained that Levenstein, accepted by laborers as a fellow-worker and Social Democrat,[5] had gathered data--admittedly unrefined-- from the workers that was unavailable to the social scientists of the Verein.

In an effort to impel Levenstein toward more rigorous analyses, Weber published an essay entitled: "On the Method of Social-Psychological Inquiry and Its Treatment" (1909b), that has been praised both for its sensitivity to techniques of survey research, and its attention to the construction of typologies (Lazarsfeld and Oberschall, 1965; Oberschall, 1965; Heckmann, 1979).

---

[5] The Social Democrats, at the time of Weber's writing, were closely aligned with the concerns of the working class. Weber obviously assumed that Levenstein's membership in the party enhanced his credibility with the workers. If return rates can be used as a criterion, Weber was correct in his assessment: In comparison with the Verein-sponsored study, Levenstein's return rate was 63%.

After describing the circumstances surrounding the material, Weber engaged in a methodological critique of Levenstein's study. Primarily, the volume of information was so great (as opposed to the Verein study), that Weber was unclear regarding the criteria of selection for inclusion in the analysis:

> ...as the examination now exists, it remains total-
> ly unclear as to what sort of pattern (Typus) the
> total material represents, especially to what extent
> they are a "selection" and according to which
> viewpoints: whether there is a quality-selection or
> a selection of "characteristics" (and in what sense
> characteristics?) (Weber, 1909b:154).

In view of this, Weber called for a team of experts to analyze only a portion--approximately 1/12--of the data, although he did not specify the criteria for selection of the "relevant" data. However, Weber detailed recommendations for increasing precision and understanding of the material:

> ...it requires extreme caution to clarify and com-
> plete unclear or neutral answers; and particularly,
> the analysis of the motive requires the greatest di-
> ligence to ascertain its special characteristic
> (Abschattierung) and to establish combinations of
> the same that cannot, of course, be ascertained by
> "enumeration" alone... (Weber, 1909b: 157-158).

Weber also argued, in this essay, for the _inductive_ derivation of typologies. Lazarsfeld and Oberschall (1965) and Heckmann (1979) have remarked that this procedure was at variance with his construction of ideal types. However, this mode of typological construction was only one of several methods that Weber utilized in the formation of ideal types. For purely methodological purposes, he did not divorce concrete, empirical data from historical evidence during any period of his writing.[6] Weber (1908a:396) clearly expressed this point in an essay discussing the role of ideal types in the analysis of economic phenomena.

This essay also marked the last completely developed effort by Weber to engage in empirical research. One later effort, a study of the distribution of power in the German press, ended with Weber's withdrawal from the project. This development was unfortunate, as it would have been Weber's first empirical research in a study completely independent from the constraints of the Verein. Additionally, it would have employed Weber's notion of value-freedom within concrete empirical research of historical data (cf. Heckmann, 1979:60). In preparation for the study, Weber (1910, in 1924b) wrote an essay detailing the procedures for a content-analysis of the work [...and from these quantitative findings, we can proceed to the qualitative determinations (Weber, 1910 in 1924b:440) R]. Thus, had the study reached its completion under Weber's direction, it would almost certainly have progressed along the lines of Weber's earlier efforts. The lines of development of the proposed study demonstrated adherence to the postulates of

---

[6] Interestingly, Oberschall has recognized this point in another work (Oberschall, 1965:121n).

his methodological writings and developing new techniques for empirical investigation.

WEBER'S LAST METHODOLOGICAL WRITINGS

In 1913, Weber returned to more abstract methodological formulations, with the publication of an article entitled: "Some Categories of Interpretive Sociology."[7] The essay has been cited as Weber's "first systematic statement of his own sociology [and] is an indication of the evolution of Weber's thought (Graber, 1981:145). Winckelmann (in Weber, 1973b) has remarked that: This methodological and classificatory contribution to the concepts of sociology contains in nuce the entire focus of...Weber's interpretive sociology." The essay was a "summary" statement of Weber's methodology, and it served as the basis for the methodological introduction to Economy and Society (Roth, in Weber, 1978a:xciv).

Weber began the exposition by arguing for the importance of Verstehen: "An 'understanding' ('Verstaendnis') of human behavior achieved through interpretation contains, to varying degrees, above all a specific 'self-evidence'" (Weber, 1913 in Weber, 1981:151). However, Weber, quickly divorced his concept from that of the intuitionists, rejecting Verstehen as a method in

---

[7] An examination of an exchange of letters between Weber and his publisher reveals that the article was at least partially completed several years earlier, but was left unpublished until 1913.

itself, and linking its significance to the enhancement of empirical investigations:

> That an interpretation possesses this self-evidence in especially high measure still proves nothing in itself about its empirical validity...Rather, the "understanding" ("Verstehen") of the context must always be verified, as far as possible, with the usual methods of causal attribution before any interpretation, however plausible, becomes a valid "intelligible explanation" (Weber, 1913 in Weber, 1981:151).

This was precisely Weber's contention in his earlier empirical works and in the remaining part of the first section of the essay, Weber attempted to clarify the relation of Verstehen to the "gray area" to which he had referred in the "Psychophysics" paper. Weber stressed once again that there are behaviors that are more comprehensible than others. The category of behavior most readily understandable Weber termed "zweckrationales Handeln" (instrumentally rational action): "...behavior exclusively oriented to means (subjectively) considered to attain goals (subjectively) clearly comprehended" (Weber, 1913 in Weber, 1981:151). Weber then posited that instrumentally rational action very often constitutes the most appropriate "ideal type" for sociological investigation. Thus, in terse language and in the space of a few pages, Weber clarified the nexus between Verstehen and social action expressed as an ideal type.

Further, Weber rejected any direct connection between "interpretive" (verstehende) sociology and psychological forms of explanation (cf. Graber, 1975). A sociologist, Weber asserted, is interested in "meaningful relations to objects." [8] It is through examination and understanding of the external behavior of individuals to objects in terms of their actions, which can then be assessed in terms of the rationality or "irrationality" of the behavior:

> ...the more an action is appropriately oriented toward the type of correct rationality, the less the meaningful intelligibility of its course is enhanced by any psychological conditions whatsoever (Weber, 1913 in Weber, 1981:154).

For sociology, understanding social relationships both begins and ends with an examination of external behavior (Weber, 1913 in Weber, 1981:157). Weber then entered into a discussion of the importance of "objective possibility" and "adequate causation" as determined by the researcher, to examine the "correct rationality" of the action.[9]

What is "rational," and how various forms of "rationality" are combined into ideal types, Weber posited, has its basis in social values. Thus, the "value-relevance" of the neo-Kantians was made explicit: "Our work is determined by the value assumptions that support both the kind of ideal types we use and their function" (Weber, 1913

---

[8] "Meaningful conduct," for Weber, "is identifiable as such only by reference to the values expressed by the actors who engage in this conduct" (Oakes, 1975:33).

[9] However, Weber failed to fully explicate, in this essay, the necessary connection between objective possibility, adequate causation, and the construction of ideal types.

in Weber, 1981:157). Assumptions regarding the existence of certain values are accepted by the researcher, including the assumption that the social action to be examined must be "meaningful" on the parts of individuals. Sociological concepts (e.g., ideal types), are only descriptive mechanisms that allow for explanation of social action; apart from this, Weber posited, they have no meaning. This allowed him another avenue to attack the empty formalism of "organic positivism" (cf. Martindale, 1959), that had mired the social sciences in the Methodenstreit:

> The "as if" assumption is thus merely the basis of sociological inquiry...however, the subsequent conceptual development is...distinct. All analogies to the "organism" and to similar biological concepts are doomed to sterility (Weber, 1913 in Weber, 1981:167).

Although Weber did not establish the connection here, Marx's appeal to the "actions of social classes" also was a subject of this critique in other essays (e.g., Weber, 1905 in Weber, 1949:68-69).

On the basis of these methodological postulates, Weber derived a series of concepts that served to illustrate the procedure for developing an "interpretive" sociology. Although Weber intended them, in this essay, to be illustrative concepts, nearly all the concepts were employed--either explicitly or implicitly--in Weber's substantive writings. An inventory of the concepts explicated by Weber in the "Categories" essay is presented in Appendix C.

Weber's writings, following the publication of this essay, were primarily substantive essays on religion, the political order in Germany, and the preparation of his final work, Economy and Society. However, at the urging of his colleagues--notably Rickert--Weber attempted to rework "Some Categories of Interpretive Sociology." The essay, while generally well received, was criticized as being unduly abstruse. The result was a refined version, which was then included in Part I of Economy and Society. This was one of the few instances that Weber found himself forced to revise his writings, and there is some evidence to suggest that, in the case of the "Categories" essay, he found the revision to be in part counterproductive:

> As compared to the author's ("Categories") essay...the terminology (in the Economy and Society revision) has been simplified as far as possible and hence considerably changed in order to render it more easily understandable. The most precise formulation cannot always be reconciled with a form that can readily be popularized. In such cases the latter aim has had to be sacrificed (Weber, 1920 in Weber, 1978:3).

However, several important additions and clarifications were introduced in this "simplified" version. Regarding his notion of the meaning of Verstehen, Weber compared his conceptualization to that of Jaspers, Rickert, and Simmel, while notably excluding reference to the phenomenologists. Weber clarified this concept further, positing that there are two categories of Verstehen: that which is "direct observational understanding" of an act; and an "explanatory form of understanding" that involves grasping an actor's _motives_, and placing it in a larger context of meaning. Also, Weber distinguished between two types of meaning: (1) the "actual existing meaning" of an individual; and (2) a "theoretically conceived 'pure type' attributed to the hypothetical actor or actors" (Weber, 1920 in Weber, 1978:4).

Additionally, Weber clarified his stance regarding what has been termed "methodological individualism." By examining the methods of "verstehende" sociology, in comparison with Spann's "universalistic method," Weber (1920 in Weber, 1978:17-18) argued that not only are both methods indispensable, they are inseparable for a complete sociological analysis of any social action. Moreover, Weber asserted, as constitutive of a "preliminary orientation to problems," Spann's method was identical to Rickert's notion of value-relevance.

Finally, Weber augmented his explication of social action by creating his four-fold typology, ranging from instrumentally-rational action to habitual action (Weber, 1920 in Weber, 1978:24-25). This constituted a significant improvement over the discussion in the "Categories" essay. It demonstrates, further, that Weber was involved in an effort to clarify and systematize his methodological position. Baumgarten (1964:553) has related that, had Weber not been severely admonished by his students not to do so, he intended further explication of his emerging program in a series of lectures. However, in yielding to their demands, the comments in _Economy_ _and_ _Society_ were the last that would be written, as a result of his untimely death in 1920.

PART II

TOWARD A WEBERIAN METHODOLOGICAL PROGRAM

FOR THE SOCIAL SCIENCES

The historical examination of Weber's methodological writings confirms the assertions by many authors that Weber left his methodological program incomplete (see, e.g., Parsons, 1949; Tenbruck, 1959; Marianne Weber, 1975; Burger, 1976). However, after examination of the development of Weber's thought, it also becomes evident that Weber was constantly engaged in attempts to modify, refine, and expand his methodology, both in his research efforts and his more abstract methodological arguments.

Largely as a result of his critical reaction to the Methodenstreit and the Werturteilstreit, as well his involvement with the Baden neo-Kantians, Weber's methodological thought underwent a dramatic metamorphosis. As a result, he moved from a position that identified the objectives of the social sciences with the policies of the state, toward the development of an extensive complex of values. These values linked, e.g., the process of concept formation with the value orientations of both the researcher and subject, while maintaining the seemingly contradictory position that "value freedom" could be preserved in the social sciences.

Additionally, Weber's concept of "Verstehen" originated in his early research efforts, as a concern for the inclusion of the "subjective meanings" of actors. In opposition to the extremes of both organic positivism and phenomenology, Weber's notion of Verstehen gradually evolved into a necessary component of an empirically-based social science. In his early research, Weber began with an attempt to discover "ideal patterns" (Idealschemen), and gradually developed out of this the concept of the ideal type. The advances Weber made with this concept reflect a concern for value relevance, discovering a basis for establishing historical equivalents in comparative research, and the appropriate logical foundation for causal explanation in the social sciences.

However, the increasing complexity and sophistication evinced in the progression of Weber's methodological thought does not imply that his efforts resulted in a correspondingly systematic methodological program. Weber's last writings do not demonstrate any more appreciable concern for the integration of the entire body of his arguments, concepts, and procedures for empirical investigation, than did his earliest works. Systematization of his own methodological program was rarely Weber's primary concern; for this reason, it must become the central focus for those who hope to clarify his attempts, and address the possibilities for the application of his methods. Given the historical developments to which Weber was responding, the primary intellectual influences on his methodological thought, and a knowledge of the lines along which he developed this thought, it becomes possible to outline the structure of a "Weberian" methodological program.

In an effort to facilitate this task, the structure of this program has been separated into three categories: methodology, methodological concepts, and empirical method. This constitutes, of course, a significant departure from Weber. However, the distinction is necessary to articulate often intricate formulations: Weber's methodology remains one of the most complex efforts to arrive at a position that is both distinct from and yet not contrary to the empiricism of the natural sciences (cf. Graber, 1975).

The three categories that have been created are both interrelated and logically inseparable. The basis for their construction will be explicated, both by additional reference to Weber's works, and to subsequent reviews of his efforts.

An outline of the structure of the methodological program, which illustrates the progression of the stages of a Weberian research program, is presented in the diagram

below, and explained briefly in the following summary. This
provides the basis for a Weberian methodological program,
which will be proposed in chapters four, five, and six.

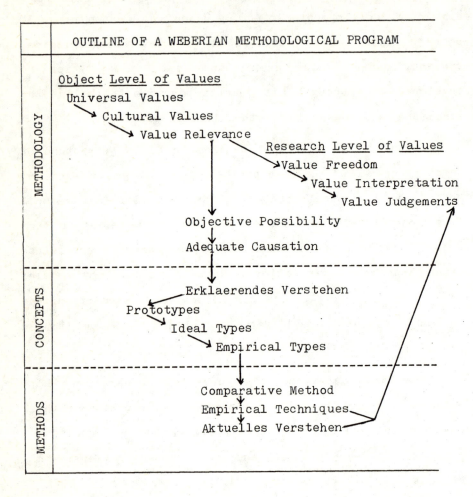

The existence of a methodological hierarchy of values in Weberian thought has been suggested by Bruun (1972). This hierarchy begins with the highly abstract assumption of "universal" (transcendental) values, and extends to concrete research activities, which are completed with the empirical assessment of individual value judgements. The first three levels of values--universal values, cultural values, and value relevance--are concerned with the axiological status of values in the social sciences, and the nexus between the selection of values and the theoretical interests of the social scientist. This is termed the object level of values. The second level of values, the research level, includes value freedom, value interpretation, and value judgements.[1] These values are related to the methodological significance of the research act itself.

Thus, the assumption of universal, transcendental values represents one of Weber's most fundamental links to the neo-Kantian position. Such values as "freedom" or "rationality" (Weber's emphasis was on the latter value) exist independently of the direct perception of the senses. In Weber's words, it is not that these values "should" exist, they merely do exist. Ultimately, this forms the justification for the objectivity of the social sciences.

---

[1] Bruun (1972) was the first to conceptualize a clear distinction between the object and research levels in Weber's methodological thought.

These universal values may be observed in various cultural manifestations, and thus become the initial "raw data" with which the social scientist is concerned. For example, rationality may be found in highly developed legal or economic systems in one culture; and in an emphasis on the development of religious beliefs and rituals in another culture. Because the expression of cultural values is both extensively and intensively infinite, the researcher, by virtue of his interests (Weber termed these "value-ideas"), selects those values that are seen as essential in terms of these interests. Once the relevant cultural values are selected, however, they are not seen as existing as either positive or negative entities (thus, the common-sense notion of "progress" would be inadmissible). From this perspective, the relevant values are then interpreted through the assessment of the value judgements of individuals.

Objective possibility and adequate causation are also central to Weberian methodology, as they form the basis for the beginning of a set of concepts that further define the research. As the relevant values are isolated, the importance of certain phenomena that explain the existence of values must be ascertained. This is accomplished by: (1) isolating any phenomenon that is believed significant; (2) mentally abstracting it from the nexus of related phenomena; and (3) assessing the possibility that, without its occurrence, the relevant value or values would be altered. This is what Weber meant by objective possibility-- "possible" to distinguish it from "probable" or "accidental", and "objective" because it is based on what he termed "rules of experience" (Erfahrungsregeln), or the researcher's knowledge of the basic progression of the relevant events. With repeated use of this procedure, a more complete account of the relevant phenomena can be discerned. "Adequate causation" (a German legalistic formulation), occurs with the isolation of a number of objective possibilities, and allows the researcher to conceptualize the full scope of the problem.

Based on this broad conceptualization, a series of concepts can be developed. This involves the first of two Weberian notions of understanding, termed "erklaerendes Verstehen." From this conceptualization of the problem, the researcher is able to construct "prototypes" of what will become constituted into ideal types. Thus, e.g., a pattern of concrete historical occurrences became the basis for Weber's ideal type of the bureaucracy. These ideal types, then, refer to specifiable empirical (existing) types, which may be measured in terms of their deviation from, or increasing conformance to, the ideal types.

This measurement has often been ignored in accounts of Weber's methodology. This process begins with the comparative method, in which empirical types may be compared with other empirical types, or with one or more ideal types. This is accomplished through the use of standard techniques of measurement. However, the research act is not completed until these assessments can be reduced to the meanings of individuals. These meanings can be ascertained through an examination of value judgements, which contain both a behavioral and a motivational component. Thus, both empirical techniques, as well as Weber's second notion of understanding of the actor's motives, are utilized. Aktuelles Verstehen, then, is more than assessing the "face validity" of empirical techniques, but is actively engaged in the formation and revision of these techniques. Thus, it is possible to discern, in a Weberian methodology, the existence of a complex relationship of methodological justifications, concepts, and empirical techniques for the assessment of various social phenomena.

CHAPTER IV

METHODOLOGY

The consideration of "methodology" apart from any actual historical or empirical applications, is consistent with Weber's use of the term: "the science of science" (Weber, 1913). More recently, Theodorson and Theodorson (1969:254), distinguishing "methodology" from "method," have defined sociological "methodology" as:

> ...the analysis of the basic assumptions of sociology [including] the process of theory construction, the interrelationship of theory and research, and the procedures of empirical investigation. Methodology is not concerned with building substantive knowledge, but rather deals with the procedures by which knowledge is built--conceptual, logical, and research procedures.

VALUES IN SOCIAL SCIENCE METHODOLOGY

The problem of values constituted Weber's point of departure in the development of a unique social science methodology, and formed his closest link to the neo-Kantians, particularly Rickert. Iggers (1968:160) has stated that: "Two central concerns of Rickert run through all of Weber's major essays on the methodology of the social sciences, written between 1903 and 1920--the question of values in the social sciences, and the problem of formulating a rational methodology for the study of cultural phenomena."

Within the neo-Kantian framework that Weber adopted, "value," in its widest sense, can either be a subjectively-based criterion for selection; or an unconditional universal standard--i.e., a transcendental value that is not directly apprehended by the senses (cf. Willey, 1978:23). In his elaborate explication of the problem of values in the social sciences, it is clear that Weber included both these meanings in his conceptual scheme. There are, as a result, six fundamental types of values that must be recognized by the social scientist. These values relate either to the construction of an analytic concept, to the foundation of a non-relativistic methodology, or, in the case of value-judgements, to the subject of empirical investigations.

"Universal" Values

In postulating the existence of transcendental, universal values, Weber, following Rickert, avoided the possibility that his methodological position would be associated with historical relativism (Willey, 1978:152). Thus, Weber conceived of "universally held values (or cultural concerns) whose embodiment is...approached in actually existing phenomena" (Burger, 1976:41). In this manner, while maintaining that divergent cultural perspectives of any given "universal" value exist, Weber asserted that social scientists with dissimilar cultural perspectives or backgrounds, but utilizing the same techniques of investigation, could realize the validity of the "proof" supplied. This would hold true even if the unique value-position from which it was apprehended were totally alien. The limitations imposed by historical and cultural variations were thus transcended (Oakes, 1982:610-611), and Weber (1949:58-59) could assert that "...these highest 'values' underlying the practical interest are and will always be decisively significant in determining the focus of analytical activity...[and] can lay claim to validity as empirical truth."

Such a bold assertion regarding the nature of the reality with which social scientists are concerned is rarely evinced in Weber's writings. However, it demonstrates the strength of his commitment to a Kantian framework, and the avoidance of relativism in the social sciences. Although universal values were not amenable to empirical investigation, they form the basis from which the remainder of a Weberian system of values proceeds.

Cultural Values

Weber recognized that, in social life, the "...different domains of value are entwined and entangled in virtually every single important attitude that real men adopt" (Weber, 1978b:77). He also asserted that universal values cannot be directly addressed by the social scientist--to do so invites an unacceptable reification of the concept of "value." Thus, Weber's position was again consonant with that of Rickert (1926), who argued, for example, that while "progress" may exist as a transcendental value, it cannot be directly apprehended by the social scientist, except as an expression of "historical development:" Because social scientists cannot objectively assess the validity of transcendental values, they can only ["...take cognizance of the fact that certain values are actually accepted as valid (i.e., held by members of a society), but they can never determine whether a series of changes means progress or regress" (Rickert, 1926:95) S]. Weber, examining the various forms and causes of "rationality" within societies, utilized this concept as his principle initial explanatory vehicle, contending that this constituted the appropriate method of assessing societal "progress" (Weber, 1949:21; cf. Gerth and Mills, 1975; Zeitlin, 1968).

However, as cultural values are the expressions of these transcendental values, they become objects of interest for the social scientist, and lie "behind the functional purposes" of social life (Weber, 1975a:199). Music, for example, has a certain "aesthetic value" for members in all known cultures, although tonal differentiation, octave ranges, chromatic harmonics, etc., vary widely from culture to culture. What may appropriately be investigated--and what is of theoretical interest for the researcher--are the reasons for the concrete expressions of these values: what lines of development the values have taken, how they are related to the development of other aspects of the culture, and why these differ from the values inherent in other societies. Weber explored this development in a detailed essay entitled: "The Rational and Social Foundations of Music" (1958). However, perhaps his point was made more succinctly in an exposition on art:

> The total separation of the domain of values from the empirical sphere is typically revealed in the fact that the use of a particular technique, however "advanced," implies nothing at all about the aesthetic value of the work of art...from the point of view of an empirical, causal inquiry, it is precisely changes in "technique" that constitute the most important generally determinable factor in the development of art (Weber, 1978b:97).

The cultural value with which Weber was primarily concerned throughout his career was that of rationality (Bennion, 1933:47-48; Tenbruck, 1974:313; Butts, 1977:239; Brand, 1979:7). Weber defined the term broadly, to include the "rationality" of individuals as well as cultural institutions. It is utilized in a special sense by Weber to designate a general concern with increasing "calculability," "precision," or "regulation" (cf. Antonio, 1978:895; Dieckmann, 1967:3; Marianne Weber, 1975:139). Rationality is also of a primarily "scientific-technical," "metaphysical-ethical," or "practical" nature (Roth and

Schluchter, 1979). Thus, Weber's concepts and interests were not entirely intended to be a parallel concern with the philosophical concept of rationality, which can be traced from Pythagoras and Plato through the rise of neo-idealism. In this usage, the concept connotes the cultural value of intellectual and deductive ability to obtain knowledge (Lecky, 1897:16-17; Runes, 1962:263; Freund, 1968:21).

Through the cultural value of rationality, Weber was also able to describe the dynamics of rationality, by utilizing the closely associated (but not identical) concept of "rationalization" ("Rationalizierung"--cf. Kalberg, 1980). Thus, Weber (1904-1905; 1922) described the changes in societies as a result of increasing rationalization. It is at the level of cultural values then, that a Weberian methodological program would proceed to describe changes or conflicts in values through rationalization, and the possible consequences of these changes or conflicts.

Value Relativity

Weber also completely accepted Rickert's claim that, as a result of the extensive infinity of social reality, the selection of the elements for investigation becomes critical:

> Because of the logical impossibility of (attaining)
> an exhaustive reproduction of even a limited aspect
> of reality, this (necessitates the need for deter-
> mining) knowledge of those aspects of reality that
> we regard as essential because of their individual

peculiarities (Weber, 1975b:57).

For Weber, as well as for Rickert, the decisive criteria for what is finally determined to be important, are the values (Weber also termed these "value-ideas") of the individuals engaged in the investigation of social life:

> [A minute part of the respective individual reality becomes of salient interest to us through our conditioned value-ideas. These alone have meaning for us; they are important because they alone indicate the conditions that form our own interest in the problem as a result. Only because and insofar as this is the case, are the individual characteristics worth knowing (Weber, 1924b:175) T].

At this juncture in his methodological discussion, Weber began the conceptual transition from what Bruun (1972:104) has termed the consideration of the <u>object</u> level, to the <u>research</u> level.[2] It is also evident that Weber rejected the related notions of Dilthey and Husserl, that it is the task of the social scientist to understand social reality from the perspective of the actor, rather than from that of the researcher.[3] Weber acknowledged that the investigator must not only have prior knowledge of the values of those he wishes to study, but also must utilize this knowledge in his investigations (Weber, 1949:152; Weber, 1978c:21). Although this postulate may now appear to

---

[2] Similarly, Oakes (1981:611) has termed this distinction one between "theoretical" values and "practical" values.

[3] Thus, Weber was in complete accord with an earlier (1892) treatise on the same subject by Simmel (cf. Oakes, 1977:11).

be self-evident, Weber intended, with the concept of value-relevance, to establish at least three positions: (1) the differentiation of social science methodology from that of the natural sciences (cf. Oakes, 1975:33); (2) the identification of a nexus between abstract values and social action as a necessary starting point for the social scientist in an effort to interpret the expression of concrete values (Weber, 1978b:87-88); and (3) the relationship of the values of the social scientist to the object of his investigation. Although Weber did not provide a systematic elaboration of the concept of cultural relevance, choosing instead to refer the reader to Rickert's discussion (Weber, 1949:21), it is nevertheless evident that he intended this to be of central importance in his methodological scheme.

Value-Judgements, Value-Interpretation, and Value-Relevance

Weber reached his position regarding the status of concrete values, at the point at which the value-relevance of any phenomenon can be ascertained by the researcher. This position entails two aspects. One is related to the constraints imposed on the researcher; the other is in regard to the status of value-judgements (Werturteilen), which are exercised by those whom he intended to investigate. As Bruun (1972:28) has asserted:

One of the most ineradicable misunderstandings

current among Weber's critics was that of supposing
that "value-freedom," as defined by him, entailed
the impossibility of making values an object of
scientific study; in other words, that the object
level as well as the research level was to be kept
free of value judgements.

Thus, the task of the objective researcher is not to
establish values, but to examine their meanings. This, Weber
(1949:21) stated, is the task of "value-interpretation." In
this manner, Weber re-established the "Kantian dualism"--the
distinction between the "is" and the "ought," in the
methodology of the social sciences.

Although Weber failed to posit a general definition of
"value," it is clear that his discussions of this term at
the research level included two essential elements: an
intention or commitment, that is then expressed in social
action (cf. Bruun, 1972:36; Munch, 1975:63). Consequently,
Weber (1917 in Weber, 1949:1) defined the most basic "value
judgements" as "practical evaluations of the unsatisfactory
or satisfactory character of phenomena subject to our
influence." "Value-judgements," in the Weberian sense, are
thus distinguishable from various related terms--e.g.,
"norms" (Weber, 1949:152); "meanings and motives" (Weber,
1975b:152; cf. Howe, 1978:381; Munch, 1957:29; Heckmann,
1983:47; Helle, 1984:5); "ethical imperatives" and "moral
action" (Weber, 1978c:82), "eudaemonistic principles" (cf.
Willey, 1978:27); "ideals" (cf. Ferrarotti, 1982:55);
"purposes" (cf. Leat, 1972:33); or "preferences" (cf. Falk

and Hynes, 1980:102).

The separation of value-types into object and research levels, resolves the apparent contradiction of maintaining that the primary objective of the social sciences is to understand the nature of values in social life, while remaining value-free. Although the investigation of social phenomena must be kept free of value-judgements, this does not negate the possibility for making informed decisions based on scientific evidence. For Weber, however, this touches on the boundary between the responsibility of the researcher as a detached scientist and the personal "ethic of responsibility" (Verantwortungsethik) that must accompany it (Weber, 1921:21; cf. Burger, 1977:172; von Schelting, 1934:7-10; Schluchter, 1971:301-306).

Thus, a researcher employing a Weberian perspective is concerned with the problem of "values" in six different forms. First, an axiomatic assumption of the existence of universal values must be established. A transcendental or universal value, although it is not directly verifiable, becomes manifest in a potentially infinite variety of cultural values. The task of the researcher, at this point, is to ascertain those values that are relevant in a selective body of phenomena. Thus, methodological concepts (e.g., ideal types), allow for the possibility of an objective analysis through an interpretation of individual value-judgements, while retaining a position apart from the values investigated. The most basic implication stated in several of Weber's works, is that the postulate of "value-freedom" must serve to inform the individual of the various possibilities for (and consequences of) social action, while allowing for the ability to engage in choices apart from the direct intervention of science. Thus, the freedom--both of science and of the individual--can be secured.

Weber's construction of methodological concepts closely parallels his progression from an abstract to a concrete examination of values. It was Weber's belief that any methodological construct in the social sciences could produce knowledge only insofar as it could be reduced to the level of individual meaning. He suggested, however, that an "individualistic system of values" could not form the point of departure for the social scientist, and that "type concepts and generalized uniformities of empirical process" were "indispensable for the beginning of the investigation of social phenomena" (Weber, 1978a:18-19). In this manner, Weber attempted to reconcile Windelband's "idiographic" and "nomothetic" principles, and to establish a methodological foundation for "Verstehen" and the "Ideal Type" based on a system of values.

OBJECTIVE POSSIBILITY AND ADEQUATE CAUSATION

The transition between Weber's exposition of the centrality of the study of values (particularly value-relevance) in the social sciences, and the development of his methodological concepts, can be accomplished through the explication of the principles of "adequate causation" and "objective possibility." With the concept of adequate causation, Weber (1904 in Weber, 1949) argued against both the notions of Meyer and Mill, which, Weber asserted, were "deterministic" and "anthropomorphic," respectively. Thus, he established a position apart from these thinkers, basing his thought largely on the development of the concept through a synthesis of natural science logic, and a legalistic definition of proof.[4]

While recognizing that the problems were complex, Weber asserted that the content of any social science that ignored the questions of "intentionality" and "causality" would be empty. Thus, his discussion of the interconnectedness of objective possibility and adequate causation constituted attempts not only to come to grips with these problems, but to arrive at a synthesis between the two (Turner, 1983:507), and to utilize the concepts of objective possibility and adequate causation as the basis for the formation of his methodological concepts of Verstehen and the Ideal Type.

Weber (1949:173) defined the general term "objective possibility" as consisting of "propositions regarding what 'would' happen in the event of the exclusion or modification

---

[4] Weber relied primarily on works by the German physiologist von Kries, and the legal scholars Ruemelin, Leipmann, and Radbruch (Weber, 1949:166).

of certain conditions." Thus, objective possibilities were
essentially "thought constructions" (Gedankenbilder), which
were imaginatively employed in order to arrive at a certain
possible set of conditions that could produce a specifiable
event. Weber further restricted the definition, by
insisting that the construction of objective possibilities
must be constrained by the "rules of experience"
(Erfahrungsregeln), and accompanied by a historical
perspective that could determine the significance of any
event in society.

Thus, this mode of thought for Weber was "objective"
because it could be distinguished from a subjective "feeling
of random expectation;" and "possible" to distinguish it
from a stronger statement of "probability." Illustrating the
need of objective possibility in order to arrive at the
"importance" of a given event for the social scientist,
Weber (1949:171) asked: What could have occurred had the
outcome of the battle of Marathon been such that the Persian
culture was able to achieve dominance over the Hellenic?
The "objective possibility" existed, Weber suggested, that
the subsequent development of Western civilization would
have been altered significantly. Without an understanding
of the significance of this possibility, "...there would in
truth be no reason why we should not rate that decisive
contest equally with a scuffle between two tribes of Kaffirs
or Indians" (Weber, 1949:172).

With the determination of the significance of a given event, selection of only those factors that are somehow "relevant" to the event remains to be discovered. Weber remarked that this was the central task of adequate causation:

> Our real task is, however: by which logical operations do we acquire the insight and how can we demonstratively establish that...a causal relationship exists between those "essential" components of the effects and certain components among the infinity of determining factors (Weber, 1949:171).

This initial task could only be accomplished by arriving at the constellation of objective possibilities that could act in unison to "cause" the event. This notion of "causality" implies not "necessity," but rather "adequacy," in the sense that the degree of causation for any event may be decided with relative degrees of certainty. The establishment of a series of causal connections, then, becomes valid "...only when it is able to pass the test of the use of the category of objective possibility which entails the isolation and generalization of the causal components for the purpose of ascertaining the possibility of the synthesis of certain conditions into adequate causes" (Weber, 1949:177).

The combination of objective possibility and adequate causation forms the immediate methodological setting for Weber's concepts of Verstehen and the Ideal Type. For example, the concept of Verstehen was important for Weber as a technique for understanding the "empirical rules" of social action. This becomes increasingly clear in his later works, beginning with his "Categories" essay in 1913 (cf. Turner, 1983). This is also true of the construction of ideal types; for example, Weber (1949:93-94), commenting on the basis for the construction of the ideal types, "church" and "sect," remarked that: "Certain characteristics of both become 'essential' <u>because</u> (it can be shown that) they stand in an adequate causal relationship."

CHAPTER V

METHODOLOGICAL CONCEPTS

Based on this methodological foundation, Weber developed an extensive typology of concepts. "Methodology," in a Weberian program, forms the rationale and procedures through which the concepts can be constructed. Thus, each abstract methodological postulate in a Weberian program finds more concrete expression in a system of concepts. Weber's notion of one of the most important of these concepts--Verstehen--has also been a source of increasing controversy (Abel, 1948; Munch, 1957; Wax, 1967; Warriner, 1969; Burger, 1977). Thus, in order to formulate a Weberian system of methodological concepts, Verstehen requires considerable clarification. Much of this clarification, however, can be achieved through a closer inspection of Weber's works.

VERSTEHEN

The distinction between "Verstehen" and other related modes of social inquiry has often been dichotomized as a difference between "Verstehen" (understanding), and "Erklaeren" (explanation--cf. Rickert, 1921; Moon, 1977;

Markovic, 1972). However, Weber stressed the importance of "Verstehen" in a manner similar to other social thinkers of his era, but also introduced into the concept elements that were directly related to Erklaeren, thus creating diverging _types_ of Verstehen. These types were utilized by Weber to accomplish two purposes: (1) the construction of a methodological tool that achieved the transition from value-relevance, objective possibility, and adequate causation to the establishment of ideal types (cf. von Schelting, 1934:325); (2) the establishment of a method for the verification of empirical results that stood apart from organic positivism.

This approach, for Weber, follows logically from his position regarding the status of the social sciences vis-a-vis the natural sciences. The additional task of understanding subjective phenomena, seen as deeply problematic for other social scientists of his era, presented for Weber a unique opportunity to grasp more fully the complex reality of the subject of investigation: "We can accomplish something that is never attainable in the natural sciences; namely, the subjective understanding of the component individuals" (Weber, 1922 in 1978a:15). Thus, the special requirement of the social sciences to isolate only the relevant values associated with a given phenomenon, and the necessity of understanding social action at the level of meaning, is indicative of the dual nature of Weber's formulation, as well as its centrality within his attempt to establish a method for the social sciences (Weber, 1924b:84, 88-89, 99, 415; Weber, 1978a:10-11,13,15).

Weber's Concept of Verstehen as Distinct from Intuitionism

The concept of Verstehen had been radically altered by Weber and others since the introduction of the term in German social science by Droysen in 1850 (Burger, 1977:166). Droysen, like later philosophers of science, had employed the term largely in response to organic positivism's increasing hold during the beginning of the Methodenstreit. The development of the concept of Verstehen, then, can be traced from the intuitionism of Droysen and Dilthey, to the more tempered empirical formulations of Simmel, Rickert, and Weber, although the contemporary controversy over Verstehen tends to center around Weber's notion alone.

Burger (1977:165) has asserted that Weber "...had little, and at any rate nothing particularly original, to say regarding the status of man's "inner states." Although somewhat overstated, this fact should not be surprising. Weber's intent lay in establishing a mode of Verstehen that did not so much supplant positivism, but attempted to augment it. Thus, Weber's attempt appeared to be more an effort to free Verstehen from its earlier "intuitionist" meaning, and to incorporate it into a larger methodological framework (cf. Baar, 1967:338).

Weber's opposition to intuitionism rested on two grounds. First, he saw no independent criteria from which to judge the correctness or incorrectness of any intuition: "As long as 'reproduction in immediate experience' remains on the plane of 'feelings,' it will produce first person value feelings that are intrinsically inarticulated" (Weber, 1975:179-180). Thus, reliance on an "intuitionist" form of Verstehen could never, in itself, produce any sort of reliable certitude, even of personal experience:

> Reflective knowledge, even of one's own experience, is nowhere and never a literally "repeated experience" or a simple "photograph" of what was experienced; the "experience," when it is made into an "object," acquires perspectives and interrelationships that were not "known" in the experience itself (Weber, 1949:178).

Secondly, Weber suggested that the emphasis by intuitionists on grasping the phenomenon in a somehow "holistic" manner leads, in reality, to the opposite result. Thus, a simplistic reconstruction would emerge that ignored several important elements:

> Causal analysis may be repressed in favor of the search for a "total character" that corresponds to the "feeling of totality." Since the need for a formula that reproduces the "synthesis of feeling" replaces the need for a formula that expresses the results of empirical analysis, this "total character" is affixed to the "epoch" like a label. Subjective, emotional "interpretation" in this form does not constitute empirically historical knowledge of real relations (Weber, 1975b:180-181).

The role of Verstehen, for Weber, was thus far removed from the sort of "re-experiencing" (Nacherleben) that Dilthey had envisioned (Hodges, 1949:111-112). As Hughes (1958:302-303) has suggested, this was another example of Weber's "neo-Kantian reliance upon conceptual rigor," rather than intuition, to establish objective knowledge in the social sciences. Although Dilthey and the neo-Kantians, including Weber, were all attempting to establish a methodology for the social sciences that was not relativistic (cf. Leff, 1971), Dilthey's total reliance on an intuitive form of Verstehen necessarily led to a position that was "fundamentally idealistic" (Martindale, 1959:64).

Thus, although it is clear that Weber had acquired a thorough knowledge of Dilthey's works (Iggers, 1968:181), and generally utilized various aspects of them as supportive illustrations in his own early methodological writings (e.g., Weber, 1975b: 84,94,216n), Dilthey's observations regarding the division of the sciences, rather than his notion of Verstehen, were the favored topics of discussion.[1]

---

[1] Although Weber did take Dilthey's intuitionism to task, it was indirectly, through critiques of Dilthey's epigoni--primarily Wundt, Muensterberg, and Croce--in which his form of Verstehen was addressed.

Relationship to Conceptualizations of Simmel
and Rickert

While Weber's account of Verstehen was often
diametrically opposed to those of the intuitionists, it
emerged in Weber's thought as a direct corollary to Simmel's
earlier (1892) formulation, although this has often been
overlooked (Helle, 1984:2). Thus, Weber (1951:93) remarked
that:

> [Within the wide range of possible meanings for the
> term "Verstehen," Simmel should be credited with
> achieving a clear distinction between the "objective
> understanding" of the meaning of a message and the
> subjective "interpretation" of the (speaking or act-
> ing) individual U].

Although it must be noted that Weber later sharply qualified
this praise of Simmel (Weber, 1978a:4), it is apparent that
he never denied his indebtedness to Simmel for much of his
own understanding of this concept (Weber, 1977:158-163).

There exists, however, an apparent irony in Weber's
thought at this point. Simultaneous with his becoming more
sharply critical of Simmel's concept of Verstehen, it
appears that Weber's own conceptualization began to more
closely parallel Simmel's notion of Verstehen.[2] Simmel's
concept was, therefore, not only prior to Weber's own

---

[2] For example, Rex (1971:30), has noted that, in Economy
and Society, "We find Weber talking about social forms
separated from their content in precisely the manner that
Simmel advocated."

discussion, but also decisive for its focus (cf. Helle, 1984).

Thus, the contradiction inherent in Weber's own works, in which Verstehen was promulgated as a tool for grasping "meaning" at the "level of the individual," but remained on the level of the formation of the concept, can be traced to several sources. Primarily, these included Weber's preoccupation with the refutation of "intuitionism;" and secondly, his emphasis on Simmel's notion of Verstehen, in an effort to discover a methodological justification for the formation of sociological concepts.

Additionally, the influence of Rickert with regard to Weber's development of the concept of Verstehen appears to have had a significant impact. Rickert (1921:424) began his analysis by stating: ["The expression "Verstehen" has many meanings...and the theories of Verstehen are as numerous as the meaning of the word" V]. The progression of Rickert's attempts to clarify and narrow the concept to the point that it could be utilized as a central method for the social sciences, once again significantly influenced Weber's thought.

Given Rickert's profound influence on other aspects of Weber's methodology, it was not surprising that Weber's explication of Verstehen paralleled Rickert's concept in at least two respects. First, Rickert's position regarding value-relevance found its methodological resolution in

Verstehen through objective possibility and adequate causation. Thus, "Verstehen," for Weber, was the methodological concept that constituted the product of these logically prior methodological considerations. Secondly, the concept of Verstehen, for both, was antithetical to any "psychologistic" interpretation. As Rickert (1921:424) stated: [...the problem of...Verstehen is not psychological; i.e., not through investigation of "inner life" alone can a solution be reached." W] Again, the influence of Rickert on Weber is unmistakable, as seen in this passage:

> When one "explains"...an action, that certainly does not mean that one will infer it from the "psychic" data. Rather, it means exactly the opposite...(Weber, 1913 in Weber, 1981:154).

Role and Limitations of Verstehen in Weberian Methodology

In sharp contrast to several of his contemporaries, then, Verstehen appears to have played a more limited role in Weber's overall methodological framework than is often realized. This is apparent at several junctures in Weber's writing, as has been shown. This has led several later authors to the false conclusion that the concept is either unimportant or that it performed contradictory functions in his methodology (see, e.g., Abel, 1948; Warriner, 1969; Burger, 1976).

However, the concept of Verstehen is central to Weber's entire methodological foundation, and it might even be asserted that it is one of the most fully-explicated concepts in his methodological corpus. The resolution of the apparent contradiction lies in the recognition that Weber intended that Verstehen should serve two totally distinct functions. First, it is meant to function as a methodological concept. Secondly, it is a method of analysis that is both particular to and separates the task of the social sciences from the natural sciences. The notion of the existence of different "types" of Verstehen that serve analytically distinct functions has often been suggested (Wax, 1967; Warriner, 1969; Munch, 1975), although it was Parsons who deciphered the essential functions of Verstehen that Weber had attempted to establish: "<u>erklaerendes</u>" (explanatory) Verstehen, and "<u>aktuelles</u>" (observational or direct) Verstehen.[3]

Erklaerendes Verstehen

As a methodological concept, "erklaerendes Verstehen," as defined by Parsons, relates to the comprehension of a particular act as understood in a "...broader context of meaning involving facts that cannot be derived from a particular act or expression" (Parsons, in Weber,

---

[3] Abel (1929) discovered the same distinction in Weber's thought, but failed to fully understand the role of erk- laerendes Verstehen in concept-formation.

1978a:58n). The role of this form of understanding is directly related to the formation of more specific concepts (e.g., the bureaucratic ideal type), that can then be used in comparative research settings. It is erklaerendes Verstehen, then, which is the concept generated from analyses of value-relevance, objective possibility, and, in Weber's words, the "rules of experience." Erklaerendes Verstehen forms, in turn, the basis for the development of ideal types (cf. Machlup, 1960:33; Ferrarotti, 1982:51).

Aktuelles Verstehen

In contrast to erklaerendes Verstehen, the second form of understanding is termed "aktuelles Verstehen." This was Weber's term to describe the form of understanding related to the direct perception of the actor's motives and actions. As it is not a methodological concept, but a method related to research, it will be discussed in the following chapter.

IDEAL TYPES, PROTOTYPES, AND EMPIRICAL TYPES

Relation of Ideal Types and Erklaerendes Verstehen

Along with the notion of Verstehen, the Ideal Type has been both widely acclaimed and criticized as a component of Weber's methodological excursus (McKinney, 1966; Hekman, 1983). Viewed as conceptually isolated from the other facets of Weber's methodology, the ideal type has been depicted as an end of Weber's research efforts. However, this is a position that Weber (1949:29) categorically rejected: "The construction of abstract ideal types recommends itself not as an end but as a means."

Ideal types form, rather, the basis for the transition from a series of methodological concepts to Weber's comparative method. As such, ideal types must be viewed as existing immediately prior to the research act, and closely connected to erklaerendes Verstehen. Ferrarotti (1982:51) has grasped this point most clearly, with his assertion that ideal types represent "...a conscious contact between 'understanding' (Verstehen) and "experiencing" (Erfahren), here synonymous with "explanation" (Erklaeren)." Thus, the "explanatory understanding" that emerged as a result of Weber's purely methodological argument finds its fullest expression in the ideal type.

Origins and Definition of the Ideal Type

Weber began his consideration of the ideal type as a result of his struggles to achieve a resolution between historical facts and historical concepts. However, with an increasing sociological focus and the methodological concerns engendered by the Methodenstreit, he expanded the role of the ideal type to include the possibility for the establishment of a basis of objectivity apart from that of the natural sciences. Weber also departed from Rickert's limited notion of the "historical individual", and moved toward the establishment of a separate concept which could be utilized in the explanation of purely social phenomena (e.g., the comparative analysis of various institutions).

The concept of the ideal type, then, constitutes a "...conceptual construct (Gedankenbild) which is neither historical reality nor even the 'true' reality...(but is) formed by the synthesis of a great many diffuse, discrete, more or less present and occasionally absent concrete individual phenomena, which are arranged according to those one-sidedly emphasized viewpoints into a unified analytical construct" (Weber, 1949:90). Much of Weber's explanation of the ideal type was constituted in the negative. Thus, the ideal type, in Weber's words, is not a "theory" or an "hypotheses," nor is it a "description of reality," an "ethical imperative," or an "average type" (Weber, 1949:90-91, 100-101; 1975a:190; 1978a:21-22). It is also not amenable to confirmation or rejection in any scientific sense since, as a heuristic concept, it must be judged only in terms of its adequacy of description.

Functions and Categories of the Ideal Type

The main functions of ideal types, then, are to provide the researcher with the means to assess their characteristics, both in relation to other constructed ideal types,[4] and the comparison of ideal types with empirical

---

[4] Weber's The Protestant Ethic has often been cited as the clearest example of this use.

reality (Weber, 1949:43; cf. Lopreato and Alston, 1970:88; Ritzer, 1983:129). For this, Weber made implicit use of several fundamentally distinct kinds of ideal types (Weber, 1949:89-107; Weber, 1978a:1215-1217), although this excursus was not often systematically developed. This has led to a plethora of attempts to "systematize," in some fashion, Weber's allusion to the existence of different forms of the ideal type to describe similar phenomena (Salomon, 1934; Parsons, 1964; McKinney, 1966; Dieckmann, 1967; Aron, 1970; Sahay, 1971; Burger, 1976). However, each of these attempts tends to reflect a series of themes underlying Weber's analytic rationale, which may be summarized along the following axes:

(1) Generalizing/Individualizing

(2) Historically-derived/Logically derived

(3) Ideal/Empirical

Each of these categories, in turn, reflects Weber's neo-Kantian position that the development of concepts--while potentially useful for apprehending social reality--do not serve as reflections of this social reality. Rather, they act as conceptual devices that describe phenomena not in their "real" forms, but only "as if" they behaved in the manner specified (Weber, 1949:102; cf. Vaihinger, 1924:314; Tenbruck, 1959:625; Dieckmann, 1967:36-37). This qualification was extremely important. With it Weber avoided the conceptual pitfall that has trapped several later

Weberian critics; i.e., the conflation of conceptual abstraction and empirical reality.

Prototypes and Empirical Types as Methodological Concepts

Systematization of Weber's ideal types, while valuable, does not lay to rest the frequent criticism that ideal types exist as _static_ concepts that are, in essence, subjectively-derived and immutable. For example, Burger (1976:120) has contended that:

> It does not seem to lead very far to argue that the term is applied to seemingly heterogeneous things which must be distinguished if one wants clarity. Rather, one must discover the reasons Weber had to treat them as the same. One must discover why it apparently was entirely natural for him...to call these things "ideal types."

For this, one cannot rely completely on either the ideal types themselves, or to the phenomena which ideal types refer. Rather, the _basis_ for the formulation of the ideal type must be specified. Unfortunately, this is absent in much of Weber's work. Hekman (1983:34) has observed that: "Weber is not always as clear as he should be on the nature of the 'reality' from which the ideal type is drawn and to which it is compared." Only through an examination of the components can the soundness of the ideal type be probed; this is particularly important in those cases when the ideal type loses its utility. Weber (1949:158) encouraged the formation of new ideal types as older ones lose their function as a heuristic device. However, he failed to indicate how this could be accomplished, and how an examination of the weaknesses of the "outmoded" ideal type could assist in their "reconstruction" in a more relevant form.

Prototypes Thus, the term "prototype" will be used to designate the collection of those elements that have been utilized by the researcher in the construction of an ideal type. With regard to Weber's work, this may often be gleaned from unpublished notes, the abundant footnotes in his texts, and other forms of documentation--e.g., Marianne Weber (1975) has related that Weber's ideal-typical "capitalist" was not a composite representation, but almost entirely a depiction of Weber's entrepreneurial uncle. When revision of an ideal type is necessary, information regarding the source of the original concept could be invaluable in a search for a more methodologically adequate "reconstruction."

Empirical Types Further, it is necessary to specify those empirical types to which the ideal type refers, since the empirical types--and not the ideal types themselves-- indicate the validity of any particular construction. However, this fact has all too often evaded critics of Weber's position.[5] Thus, ideal types must continue in their accuracy to reflect changes in the empirical types:

As Machlup (1960:54 has observed: [The conceptual pairing of empirical types and the ideal type is, in Anglo-American (sociological) literature, almost completely unknown" X].

> Either the ideal type must become modified to re-
> flect the changes of the real (empirical) type, or
> one retains the ideal type in its "pure" form, and
> it thus becomes a concept with no referent in the
> real world (Blau, 1963:311).

The explicit reference to empirical types, then, represents a step toward achieving the isomorphism between ideal types and the "rules of experience," allowing for for changes in the ideal type, in order to maintain its utility.

With the specification of empirical types, an additional criticism that has repeatedly surfaced regarding Weber's concept of the ideal type is resolvable. This criticism is exemplified by the criticism by Rex (1971), who argued that Weber developed the concept of the ideal type during the earliest years of his career, when his concerns were predominantly "historical" in nature. However, as Weber increasingly developed a sociological interest, he failed to explicate a concomitant ideal type that was in any "sociological." This argument loses its substance, however, when a distinction is established between ideal types and empirical types. Weber's initial methodological thrust was to provide a basis for the understanding of history apart from the concrete "reality" of the events themselves (empirical types), and the concept of the ideal type represents, in large part, Weber's efforts to achieve a sociological analysis through a historical perspective.

CHAPTER VI

RESEARCH METHODS

Weber's central purpose in constructing ideal types was to provide a more refined basis for establishing comparisons of similar patterns of social behavior, both within and across societies (Martindale, 1959:59). Thus, Weber (1905, in Weber, 1949:97) remarked that ideal types "...are of great value for research and of high systematic value for expository value when they are used as conceptual instruments for <u>comparison</u> with and the <u>measurement</u> of reality." In his efforts, Weber characteristically assumed the presence of some phenomena common to the "real" types corresponding to the ideal type in which he was interested. He then attempted to explain the absence of these phenomena in other real types (cf. Roth, 1971:76). Thus, Weber introduced his "classic" work, <u>The Protestant Ethic</u>, with the observation that:

> A product of modern European civilization studying any problem of universal history is bound to ask himself to what combination of circumstances the fact should be attributed that in Western civilization...cultural phenomena have appeared which...lie in a line of development having universal significance and value (Weber, 1958a:13).

COMPARATIVE METHOD

For Weber, the comparative approach, using ideal types, constitutes the completion of his evolution from a critic of traditional historical methods to that of a researcher and theorist with sociological interests (cf. Nelson, 1975:229). Weber's movement toward a comparative perspective was not, however, without serious reservations regarding its worth.[1] Nonetheless, it is this level of analysis toward which Weber increasingly turned his attention, and it ultimately became his primary focus of interest (cf. Rex, 1971), as well as the method that has subsequently received the most unqualified acclaim (Parsons, 1964:121; Vallier, 1971:6).

EMPIRICAL METHODS

"Empiricism," in a Weberian methodological framework, does not employ the term in the same sense as that of behaviorism, although an analysis of external behavior constitutes both the beginning and end points of Weber's investigations:

> ...understandable relationships and particularly rationally oriented sequences are, for sociology, thoroughly qualified to act as links in a causal chain that begins...with "external" conditions and in the end leads again to "external" behavior.

---

[1] In a letter to a colleague (1914), Weber stated that, as a comparative sociologist, he risked being labeled a "dilettante," adding that comparison of social behaviors constituted only "very modest preparatory work."

Weber's purpose, in utilizing ideal types of various historical or comparative phenomena, was not ultimately the discovery of similarities, but significant differences between these phenomena:

> [A truly critical comparison of the developmental states of the ancient polis and the medieval city...would be rewarding, but only if this comparison does not chase after "analogies" and "parallels"...in other words, it should be concerned with the distinctiveness of each of the...developments...and the purpose of the comparison must be the causal explanation of the differences (Weber, 1924b:257,288) Y].

Thus, whereas the ideal type performs a heuristic function through the aggregation of phenomena with perceived similarities into a type concept with no concrete referent in social reality, the purpose of the comparative method is the disaggregation of existing social phenomena to explain their differences. Weber's research was conducted in this manner from an early point in his career. For example, Weber's most comprehensive analysis of the ancient world, entitled "Agrarian Conditions in Antiquity" (1909a), was a comparative study of Mesopotamia, Egypt, Israel, Greece, the Hellenic realm, and Imperial and Republican Rome.

The "real types" to which the ideal types refer, then, are those entities that are compared. Despite criticism to the contrary, Weber's analyses often established this connection between ideal types and real types, although this was not always made explicit in his substantive works. For example, in his essay, "The City" (1909 in 1978a:1215-1216),

Weber developed three ideal types of cities. The ideal type of the "consumer city" was comprised of widely divergent types of consumers; e.g., officials or manorial lords. Weber listed Peking and Moscow (before the abolition of serfdom), as concrete examples of this ideal type. The cities within this one ideal type can then be compared, Weber argued, in an effort to analyze meaningful differences between them. The distinction between cities having primarily urban land rents and those with an abundance of "extra-urban" sources could be analyzed, in an effort to determine the impacts on city growth, the concentration of power, and the conditions in rural regions.

Consequently, a Weberian methodological program, following Weber's tenets, does not <u>empirically</u> "compare" ideal types. Rather, three procedures are possible, involving both the construction of ideal types and the specification of empirical (or real) types: (1) comparisons of the real type(s) within the conceptual framework of one ideal type; (2) comparisons between real types (both historical and contemporaneous) within different ideal types; and (3) comparisons between various real types and several ideal types. The possibility of judging the validity of these comparisons, then, does not rely on a return to the ideal type, but rests on techniques of measurement and aktuelles Verstehen.

Techniques of Measurement

Weber's commitment to the use of empirical techniques of measurement similar to those of contemporary sociology is readily apparent. Although the research designs and statistical procedures were often primitive by contemporary standards, both Weber's intent and his skill in developing new techniques were obvious throughout his career. For example, his preliminary design for "The Psychophysics of Industrial Work" anticipated (and in some senses surpassed), Mayo's Hawthorne experiments, which were performed over twenty years later (Oberschall, 1965).

It has been demonstrated that, although his substantive works remained largely on the level of comparative analysis (Ritzer, 1975:16; Gerth and Mills, 1975:57; Oakes, 1982:591), Weber's ultimate objective was to empirically assess the validity of these comparisons (Weber, 1913 in Weber, 1981:151), and to establish thereby a "science of concrete reality" ("Wirklichkeitswissenschaft"-- Weber, 1904 in Weber, 1949:72--cf. Bruun, 1972:94-144). Thus, Weber designed surveys, collected and analyzed data, and was in the process of developing content analysis techniques to investigate social change in a more systematic manner than merely providing historical documentation. This was illustrated by his comments regarding the study of the German press:

[We must begin by measuring, in a very pedestrian
manner, with scissors and compass, how the contents
of the newspapers have quantitatively shifted in the
course of the generation, between light literature
and editorial, between editorial and news, (and)
between what is and what is not any longer considered news (Weber, 1911b:41) Z].

AKTUELLES VERSTEHEN

An analysis of this order, however, does not comprise

the final stage of research for an "interpretive" sociology.

There must also be a reciprocal exchange between analyses of

secondary data (such as in the German Press Study), and a

more direct understanding of the value-judgements of

individuals. Thus, Weber remarked at one point that:

> ...the relevance for interpretive sociology of
> processes devoid of "subjective meaning"
> ("Sinnbezogenheit")--as, say, the course of vital
> statistics, the selection processes of anthropologi-
> cal types, or, say, the course of vital statistics,
> or, of purely psychic facts--lies exclusively in
> their role as "conditions" and "consequences" toward
> which meaningful action is oriented, just as climat-
> ic or botanical conditions are relevant for economic
> theory (Weber, 1913 in 1981:153).

As Parsons (1978a:58n) has stated, aktuelles Verstehen

for Weber constituted "...the possibility of deriving the

meaning of an act or symbolic expression from immediate

observation without reference to any broader context." Thus,

this type of Verstehen differs from erklaerendes Verstehen,

as it does not serve as a method for concept construction,

but for providing the basis for the determination of meaning

at the level of the individual. As opposed to intuitionism,

then, this effort is not a "complete" method, but a necessary step in validating the findings of empirical research:

> Explanations of concrete behavior in terms of its meaning are, even with the highest degree of self-evidence, only explanatory hypotheses for sociology. They therefore need to be empirically verified in essentially the same manner as does every hypothesis. They are valid as useful hypotheses when we may assume a measure of probability (widely varying in the individual case) that subjectively "meaningful" motivational links are present.

Weber has been criticized for this position by phenomenological sociologists (Schutz, 1967), for attempting to "scientize" the concept of Verstehen, and by positivists (Abel, 1948; Lazarsfeld and Oberschall, 1965), for attempting to interject an unverifiable or "redundant" concept into social scientific method. However, both sides of this critique have failed to grasp the fact that Weber intended this form of Verstehen as an integral component of his social science method. Aktuelles Verstehen is, as Weber asserted, a necessary, but not sufficient, method for the social sciences. As has been shown, Weber posited that certain types of behaviors (i.e., those that are instrumentally rational), are more "understandable" than less "goal-oriented" behaviors, although all types of behavior are in some sense "understandable."

It is also not the case, as has been argued (see, e.g., Winch, 1958:12), that Weber was merely "checking" Verstehen with quantitative techniques. A far more plausible assertion regarding Weber's intent is that Weber designed his instruments for quantitative research utilizing the knowledge gained through aktuelles Verstehen, and in turn attempted to better "understand" the behavior through analysis of empirical data. For example, Weber stated at one point that: "Sociology must reject the assumption that "understanding" ("Verstehen") and causal "explanation" have no relationship to one another. It is true that they begin their work at opposite poles of events" (Weber, 1913 in 1981:157).

Moreover, it is clear that, for Weber, the isolation of a "fact" in the social sciences was predicated on an understanding of the meanings of individuals in the context of social action and that the "understanding" of this fact was not founded on quantitative evidence alone: "The statistical frequency of a behavior in no way makes its meaning more 'understandable,' and optimum 'comprehensibility' is not necessarily correlated with frequency; indeed, in the case of pure subjective instrumental rationality, there is often a negative correlation" (Weber, 1913 in Weber, 1981:157). Thus, a Weberian program for social science would be incomplete if the analysis failed the test of adequacy at the level of meaning for individuals. Aktuelles Verstehen is more than indicating the "face validity" of empirical data, as it relies less on logical consistency, while placing more emphasis on intersubjective understanding and the generation of new hypotheses for investigation. In this function, aktuelles Verstehen constitutes the final and definitive research act in a Weberian methodological program for the social sciences.

CHAPTER VII

CONCLUSION: SIGNIFICANCE OF A WEBERIAN

METHODOLOGICAL PROGRAM

The historical development of Weber's methodological
works has been presented, focusing attention on the
development of his methodological arguments, concepts, and
empirical applications of these from the inception of his
career in 1889 until his death in 1920. Based on this
analysis, a preliminary methodological program for the
social sciences has been proposed, which postulates the
centrality of several different aspects of values expressed
in social action, and Weber's concern for an objective
scientific approach capable of analyzing these values. The
assumption underlying the purported significance of this
book, then, is that Weber's methodological tale has not been
fully told, nor has its implications been fully realized.

IMPORTANCE OF UNDERSTANDING WEBER'S METHODOLOGICAL WRITINGS

Given Weber's standing in contemporary sociology, a
thorough knowledge of his methodological corpus should have
intrinsic importance for this reason alone. Thus, it is
curious that so little effort has been expended in analyses
of the works, particularly those that have somehow been

assigned a "secondary" importance. This is not only true in American sociology: Although von Schelting's (1934) classic work was published over fifty years ago in Germany, the procession of subsequent writings regarding Weber's methodology have often been either tendentious or polemical. For example, Weber's nationalism (expressed both in his early methodological writings and later political essays), and his emphasis on value-freedom in the social sciences, have been falsely construed as a type of "proto-Nazism" and "decisionism," respectively.

As a result of either past neglect or distortions, then, an adequate understanding of Weber's methodological works has begun to assume a renewed importance. This understanding must begin with an historical account. Thus, in his dissertation and Habilitationschrift, Weber began an investigation of the development of various social phenomena by means of a comparative approach. Through his association with the _Verein_ _fuer_ _Sozialpolitik_, Weber then became closely involved in several empirical investigations, and with his ability to analyze and interpret the resultant data, Weber quickly emerged as a leading figure in German empirical research.

However, while his abilities impressed his contemporaries, Weber also acquired an acute recognition of the limitations of these research efforts. First, they did not appear to tap the "subjective states" of individuals, which Weber thought imperative. Members of the lower classes, particularly, were often judged to be incapable of expressing these states, and thus were not queried. Additionally, the organic positivism that characterized much of the thinking of Weber's era completely ignored phenomena such as thought, feelings, and motives, in favor of more tangible evidence.

Secondly, it did not appear that the empirical evidence gathered allowed Weber a basis for comparing structural aspects of social reality in the same manner as had his "ideal patterns" in the dissertation and Habilitationschrift. Nor did it allow him the freedom to conduct comparisons of historical events or processes in the same manner.

These problems, coupled with his increasing preoccupation with the concerns of the Methodenstreit and Werturteilstreit, "forced" Weber (as he complained in one letter), to become a methodologist. The unique solutions he proposed were an outcome of his close alliance with the Baden neo-Kantian group, as well as other neo-Kantians such as Simmel. The polemics in which Weber engaged formed the basis for the outlining of a more positive methodological program. Weber's methodological arguments, beginning with his essays on Roscher and Knies in 1902, evinced a sophisticated effort to resolve both the crises of "methods" and "values," as well as the less abstract problems inherent in methodological research.

Further, comprehension of Weber's methodological writings provides avenues towards resolving often diametrically opposed critiques in the vast body of secondary literature that has emerged. For example, the debate regarding the methodological status of Verstehen can be largely dismissed, as both sides have emphasized one part of the function of Weber's concept, while ignoring its broader methodological implications. This debate, characterized by the exchange between Abel and Wax (Abel, 1949; Wax, 1967--cf. Truzzi, 1974), the concept of Verstehen, in Weber's thought, is seen to be either an "extra-scientific" method capable only of generating hypotheses or "checking" empirical findings, in a manner similar to Winch's (1958) critique of Weber's concept.

The other side of the debate depicts Verstehen as Weber's main attempt to defeat naive positivism, in a manner similar to Dilthey's notion of Verstehen. It is apparent, however, that Weber's dual concepts of erklaerendes and aktuelles Verstehen were intended to serve both functions. Thus, hypotheses are generated and ideal types are formed through erklaerendes Verstehen, which, in Abel's terms, is an "extra-scientific" approach. In contrast, aktuelles Verstehen is intrinsically related to the research process. Aktuelles Verstehen is "anti-positivistic" only in the respect that it does not employ or rely on standard empirical techniques, but is a separate procedure that augments these techniques.

Similarly, the controversy regarding the role of ideal types in Weber's methodology can be resolved largely through a closer inspection of his works. It has been noted that Weber often appeared--particularly in Economy in Society-- to view ideal types as ends of research, rather than as providing the means for conducting his investigations. However, it is clear that Weber intended ideal types to be analytical tools that were utilized as preliminary steps in his social research, rather than as the end product of the research. This is clear not only in his methodological discussions of the term (e.g., Weber, 1924b:194,198-199), but in his substantive works as well (e.g., Weber, 1958a; 1978a).

Similarly, knowledge of Weber's neo-Kantian position affords an understanding of his position vis-a-vis relativism. Thus, with regard to the separation of value-judgements from scientific investigation (separation of the "ought" from the "is"), Weber suggested that the possibility exists for obtaining valid objective knowledge of the social world:

> When we distinguished in principle between "value-judgements" and "empirical knowledge," we presup-posed the existence of an unconditionally valid type of knowledge in the social sciences, i.e., that analytical ordering of empirical social reality (Weber, 1905 in Weber, 1949:63).

Thus, the charge that Weber successfully defeated deterministic or evolutionary theories only to rediscover relativism, is unfounded. Many of these criticisms of Weber have relied on inferences from his more widely-known substantive writings; however, it is his methodological works--beginning with his essays on Roscher and Knies and continuing into his discussion of "basic sociological terms" in Economy and Society-- that these arguments are most clearly expressed.

Finally, one central aspect of Weber's methodological corpus has often been ignored or completely forgotten: the fact that he was an accomplished empirical researcher. While the subject matter of the studies in which Weber engaged has now lost much of its significance, the intellectual content often provides valuable insights into Weber's methodological intent, and allows for a more informed perspective regarding the possibilities for its extension.

DEVELOPMENT OF A WEBERIAN METHODOLOGICAL PROGRAM

These methodological writings, then, may hold far more promise for systematization of a "Weberian" program for the social sciences than may have been realized. By separating the major tenets into three distinguishable stages, it is possible to demonstrate the necessary connections between Weber's most abstract methodological arguments and his concrete recommendations for empirical sociological analysis. This has been accomplished by postulating the existence of six different types of values, and delineating the functions of each for a social science methodological program.

Further, by specifying the object level of the analysis of values, and distinguishing it from the research level, it can be shown that Weber intended to verify the existence of the respective types of values in different ways. Thus, the Kantian argument for the existence of universal values is distinguished from the empirical argument for the techniques through which the existence and sociological meanings of value judgements can be perceived, compared, and evaluated. A Weberian methodological program, therefore, can serve as a "map" marking the transition from subjective meaningfulness to objective knowledge, and demonstrating the steps that have been utilized. As Sahay (1971:67) has remarked, Weber's methodology "...is not (merely) a system of techniques of survey and data analysis: It deals with the fundamental problems of scientific knowledge...Furthermore, Weber's is the only methodology in the whole of sociological thought which has explicitly (attempted to solve) the problems of sociological analysis."

UTILITY OF A WEBERIAN METHODOLOGICAL PROGRAM

However, in accordance with Weber's tenets, any social science program that claims a "Weberian" programmatic focus must necessarily demonstrate its utility through practical application and resultant modification. In a very real sense, even the most complete social science methodological formulation represents only an "ideal type" of how research could be conducted. Thus, whereas knowledge of Weber's methodological works allows for more informed judgements regarding his intent, any reconceptualization of this intent must, in order to conform to Weber's tenets, be able to demonstrate an ability to generate substantive knowledge.

Illustration: the Understanding of "Rationality" as Value and as Ideal Type

While Weber himself recognized that several meanings of his concept of "rationality" were "full of ambiguities" (Weber, 1920 in Weber, 1978a:85),[1] it nevertheless proved extremely productive for the description of various processes of increasing systemization and calculation in various societies. Gerth and Mills (1975) have termed rationalization Weber's "major" dynamic in the development and decline of civilizations.

Although Weber did not fully clarify the function of the concept in his analyses, it is apparent that he assumed its existence at several different levels of his

---

[1] For example, Brubaker (1984:2) has found that Weber employed at least sixteen different meanings of the term "rational" in one analysis of the development of capitalism and ascetic Protestantism alone. Others have also recognized this difficulty, and have attempted to clarify the concept further (e.g., Eisen, 1978; Moore, 1979; Udehn, 1981; Moore, 1984).

methodological thought, hence the constant shifts in meaning. First, the assumption must be made that all civilizations hold a "universal" value that may be called "rationality." Thus, the societal desire to create and maintain a system, and to rely upon the predictable ordering of the system, is stronger that the desire, at the societal level, to create chaos and unpredictability. In a Weberian methodological system, this is accepted as being the case, not that it <u>should</u> exist in any normative sense.[2] Secondly, there is no uniform manner in which this rationality is expressed in any society; rather, its various manifestations that are judged important must be assessed in every instance.

What becomes of special interest to the researcher, then, are the <u>forms</u> this rationality takes in a given society. Next, the research proceeds to the questions: How did these forms emerge in the society, and why do they occur in one society and not another?

This was the strategy Weber utilized in <u>The Protestant Ethic and the Spirit of Capitalism</u>. It was not that rationality fails to exist in, e.g., Oriental cultures, Weber suggested, but that a specific form of rationality-- capitalism--has emerged only in certain societies in the Occident. In an effort to assess the reasons for this

---

[2] In Weber's words, these values "seien, nicht sollen" --"are, not should" (exist).

occurrence, Weber suggested that the gradual transformation of Calvinism was one factor leading to the development of capitalism. Through the use of various historical materials--e.g., homilies by Benjamin Franklin and passages from the Bible--as well as empirical data regarding the characteristics of the major religious groups in Germany, Weber concluded that industrious work and frugality constituted the means whereby one could calculate one's chances for salvation. In the language of Weber's ideal types of rational action expressed at the level of the individual, this form of behavior is instrumentally-rational action (Zweckrationalitaet), in which the means were consciously understood by the practitioner in order to bring about certain ends. This type of social action was capable of direct understanding (aktuelles Verstehen) on the part of the researcher.

However, as a result of several factors--including the accumulation of large amounts of surplus wealth--Weber posited that a change had occurred in this type of rationality--the "means" could no longer be clearly distinguished from the "ends," and capitalism became an end in itself:

> One of the fundamental elements of modern capital-
> ism, and not only of that but of all modern culture:
> rational conduct on the basis of the idea of the
> calling was born...from the spirit of Christian as-
> ceticism (Weber, 1904-1905 in Weber, 1958:180).

The predominant form of behavior gradually became altered,

Weber suggested, from "instrumentally-rational" action to less directly understandable forms of social action, as a capitalistic spirit took on an intrinsic value:

> The Puritan wanted to work in a calling; we are forced to do so...victorious capitalism, since it rests on mechanical foundations, needs (Calvinism's) support no longer. The rosy blush of its laughing heir, the Enlightenment, seems also to be irretriev- ably fading, and the idea of duty of one's calling prowls about in our lives like the ghost of dead re- ligious beliefs (Weber, 1904-1905 in 1958:181-182).[3]

Thus, what was primarily instrumentally-rational conduct, gradually became transformed into a form of conduct that was all-encompassing, but the motives of that conduct had become "buried." Therefore, another form of understanding (erklaerendes Verstehen) was required in order to begin the discovery of causes that were not immediately apparent.

This illustration serves as a demonstration of Weber's utilization of several elements of his methodological scheme. What is more important, however, is the fact that this sort of Weberian approach, once made explicit, should not only augment claims that Weber was a "great classical thinker" whose works are "truly classics." It is true that what Weber accomplished with this methodology in The Protestant Ethic, he accomplished in a similar fashion in other works as well; e.g., the analysis of the emergence and

---

[3] Although Weber did not view his analysis as complete, he suggested that subsequent research efforts should includ- ed the significance of "ascetic rationalism" and "humanis- tic" rationalism.

subsequent rationalization of bureaucracies, as well depicting the probable consequences--both rational and irrational--of this process of rationalization.

The analysis and conclusions exhibited in Weber's fertile and exceptionally wide range of interests, then, always demonstrate elements of an underlying methodological framework--although not with the same degree of success or clarity.[4] Weber's methodological writings were often tentative or incomplete, relying on the works of thinkers such as Rickert and Windelband. However, the possibility remains that a form a "verstehende Soziologie"--which was Weber's term form his methodology--can be constructed, expanded, refined, and applied, producing results regarding the nature of social reality which demonstrate that Weber's contribution to sociology is by no means complete.

THE VALUE OF A WEBERIAN METHODOLOGICAL PROGRAM

This book has attempted to demonstrate, first, the progressions in the development of Weber's methodological thought. Secondly, while remaining incomplete, this thought allows for reconceptualizing the structure of this methodology, which remains unique for its breadth as well as its striking resemblance to contemporary research. As Sahay (1971:67) has remarked, Weber's methodology does not only

---

[4] For example, Turner (1974) has noted that Weber apparently failed to employ Verstehen, in any sense, in his analysis of Islamic saints.

extend to techniques of data gathering and analysis: "It deals with the fundamental problems of scientific knowledge...Furthermore, Weber's is the only methodology in the whole of sociological thought which has _explicitly_ (attempted to solve) the problems of sociological analysis."

Thus, a Weberian methodology is a valuable contribution to contemporary research, as it addresses both the foundation for the objectivity of sociological knowledge, and the steps to be taken in establishing the transition from subjective meaningfulness to objective knowledge. With this effort, Weber surpassed the works of other "classical" thinkers. For example, Simmel left no set of procedures that allow for the further development of a "Simmelian" sociology. Both his _Grundfragen_ and _Soziologie_ --in which Simmel tentatively addressed methodological issues--resulted in a failure to articulate a methodology for the social sciences (cf. Wolff, 1950:xxxv), and Simmel was forced to admit his "insecure foundations."

Of those commonly identified as "classical" social theorists, only Durkheim's conceptualizations approach those of Weber. With respect to the function of concepts, Durkheim took the opposite approach from that of, e.g., Marx:

> In the present state of knowledge, we cannot be certain of the exact nature of the state, of sovereignty, political liberty, democracy, socialism, communism, etc. Our method should, then require our avoidance of all use of these concepts so

long as they have not been scientifically established (Durkheim, 1895 in 1938:22).

However, this again misses the point that all concepts
possess only a heuristic function, and that their utility
lies not in their "scientific demonstration," but in their
ability to describe social reality. Further, Durkheim's
organicist approach led him to a highly "normative"
perspective, in which the "health" or "morbidity" of
societies depended upon a distribution of societal traits:

> We shall call "normal" these social conditions that
> are the most generally distributed, and the other
> "morbid" or "pathological"... (thus) the normal
> type merges with the average type and every devia-
> tion from this standard of health is a morbid
> phenomenon (Durkheim, 1895 in 1938:55-56).

These fundamental errors can be avoided with a Weberian
methodology, largely as a result of three factors inherent
in the structure of Weber's argument: (1) a consideration of
the criteria for objective knowledge in the social sciences;
(2) the development of an array of concepts based on the
recognition of the limitations inherent in their function as
descriptors of reality; and (3) attention to the development
of techniques for the assessment of the subjective meanings
of individuals.

It has been demonstrated, further, that in Weberian
methodology the investigation of "values" entails each of
these factors. Thus, with the assumption of the existence

of transcendental values,[5] the researcher may posit that "rationality" is a value that is inherent within the structure of human consciousness, and that this is expressed in a potentially infinite variety of cultural values. Thus, rationality may be expressed in the increasingly precise calculability and regulation of societal members vis-a-vis the development of bureaucracies. This cultural value, then, constitutes the initial point of interest for the researcher. Thus, the "value relevance" that is expressed refers to the theoretical interests of the social scientist vis-a-vis the selection of the general problem. If the phenomena to be studied are bureaucracies, they are neither seen, as Durkheim might suggest, as "healthy" or "morbid" aspects of the society, but must be interpreted as expressions of a particular universal value. In other words, once the subject matter has been selected, the principle of "value freedom" obtains.

With the selection of this basic subject for research, (in this case the rationality of bureaucracies), the relative importance of its various characteristics must be assigned. This may be determined through the isolation of objective possibilities. In the case of the rationality of bureaucracies, the social scientist may begin to examine

---

[5] All research endeavors involve a set of assumptions regarding the "objectivity" of the research. A further merit of this aspect of Weberian methodology is that it requires that these assumptions be made explicit.

historical or comparative instances of bureaucracies, mentally abstracting certain features from the various rational characteristics, and assessing the possibility that the absence of particular aspects (e.g., reliance on written documents) would cause the bureaucracy to become significantly altered. With the exhaustion of what the researcher perceives as the full range of objective possibilities, he arrives at the cluster of possibilities that are deemed capable of "adequately causing" the phenomenon.

At this point in the analysis, a form of understanding (erklaerendes Verstehen) of the phenomenon emerges. This was Weber's concept to describe the process of comprehending the social context in which the phenomenon occurs. On the basis of this understanding, "prototypes" may be discovered. These may be existing historical entities--e.g., Weber frequently cited the Prussian bureaucracy under Bismark. The creation of ideal types is the product of these prototypes--in this case, the "pure" rationality of bureaucracies--and is illustrated by Weber's six ideal-typical characteristics of bureaucracies (Weber, 1922 in 1978a:956-958). These ideal types, then, refer to existing "empirical types," whose deviation from--and the possible progression toward--the characteristics of the ideal type may be assessed. At this juncture of the analysis the pure "rationality" (a product or end-state) of the ideal type is distinguished from the "rationalization" (a process) of the empirical types.

The "rationalization of bureaucracies" in relation to the rational ideal type of bureaucracy is assessed through the comparative method. Thus, empirical types are compared with other empirical types and the ideal type itself. This is accomplished through standard techniques of measurement. However, "rationality" is not ultimately established until all concepts are reduced to (and validated by) meanings at the level of individuals. Thus, value judgements, which contain both an intentional and a behavioral component, are assessed through empirical techniques and a more direct form of understanding--termed aktuelles Verstehen--that does not require additional reference apart from the immediate context of individual action.[6] As Weber suggested, these individual meanings are most readily assessed if they are "instrumentally rational;" i.e., if ends and means are understandable by the researcher, and capable of articulation by the subject. In a Weberian scheme, these actions would be the most highly rational. However, it does not preclude the use of these techniques to evaluate the three remaining types of social action as posited by Weber. At this point, the research question may be answered: 'What

---

[6] For example, Weber gained several valuable insights regarding the nature of bureaucracies--including an appreciation of the function of informal networks--after working in a bureaucratic setting in a hospital during World War I.

are the effects of the rationalization of bureaucracies upon the rational actions of individuals'?

This summary, then, demonstrates one potential contribution to contemporary sociological methodology by tracing the progression of "rationality" from its expression as a universal value to its empirical assessment at the level of individual meaning. Moreover, it demonstrates the potential to link a methodological program with the process of theory construction, which reverses a trend in contemporary sociology toward a widening schism between "theory" and "method" (cf. Westkott, 1977). Thus, the contribution of Weberian methodology lies not only in the research practice itself, (which has advanced along lines not inconsistent with Weber's intent), but in the growth of substantive knowledge that is systematically and objectively developed.

Appendix A: German Quotes Translated in the Text

A Wie koennte eine allgemeine Theorie Soziologische Handelns aussehen, die zugleich dem Geist der Weberschen Soziologie adaquat ist und heutigen Anspruchen genugt?

B Discussionen und Darstellungen ueber "Beziehungen" zwischen Weber und Marx, Weber und Simmel, Weber und Parsons, etc., mussen abgelost werden von einer systematischen Wirkungs- und Rezeptions-forschung. Dadurch wuerden nich nur die Gefahren des "Vergleichs von Unvergleichbaren" gebannt, sondern zugleich wuerde erst dadurch der Blick frei fuer die tatsachliche Wirkung Max Webers, jenseits aller heroisierenden und/oder ideologiserten Verzerrung.

C ...der Versuch, an Stelle der Aneinanderreihung einiger methodologischer Gesichtspunkte eine systematische Untersuchung treten zu lassen [ist] hier ganz unterlassen worden...Es soll hier nich Logik getrieben, sondern es sollen bekannte Ergebnisse der modernen Logik fuer uns nutzbar gemacht, Probleme nicht selbst, sondern dem Laien ihre Bedeutung veranschaulicht werden (Weber, 1968:146n).

D "Zur Geschichte der Handelsgesellschaften im Mittelalter"

E Untersuchen ueber die Methode der Sozialwissenschaften und der politischen Oekonomie insbesondere.

F Die roemische Agrargeschichte in ihrer Bedeutung fuer das Staats- und Privatrecht

G ...diese freie Konkurrenz nicht den kleinbaueren Besitzern, sondern nur den Grosskapitalisten... Sie stellt in der Tat den schrankenlosesten Kapitalismus auf agrarischem Gebiet dar...und wird als Analogie schon erwaehnten Uebergriffen und Einhegungen der spaetmittelalterlichen Grundherren quantitativ und qualitativ nicht entfernt erreicht.

H ...das Bestehen eines Zusammenhanges zwischen zwei historischen Erscheinungen laesst sich nun einmal nicht in abstracto, sondern nur so zur Anschauung bringen, dass eine in sich geschlossene Ansicht ueber die Art, _wie_ dieser Zusammenhang sich konkret gestaltet habe, vorgetragen wird.

I Will man die Tendenzen der Entwicklung, immer unter dem Vorbehalt, dass sie eben nur Tendenzen sind...sie ganz rein ueberhaupt vielleicht nirgends realisiert escheinen, also in Idealbildern formulieren, so kann man, glaube ich, ohne allzu grosse Kuenheit sagen...

J Der Begriff 'Agrargeschichte' ist deshalb hier weit ueberschritten; es handelt sich um viel mehr, naemlich um eine Skizze der gesamten Wirtschafts- und Sozialgeschichte des Altertums.

K   Dies Material ist, darueber kann kein zweifel sein, ein ganz hervorragendes, wie es in aehnlicher Art auf wenigen Gebieten zur Verfuegung stehen duerfte. Aber allerdings stehen wir ihm insofern fast ratlos gegenueber, als wir bisher nicht im klaren find, wie es verarbeitet werden soll. Wer derartige Zusammenarbeitungen nie gemacht hat, kann sich von dem Umfange dieser Arbeit schlecterdings keine Vorstellung machen. Jedenfalls duerfen die Ansprueche nach dieser Richtung nur auf ein bescheidenes Mass gestellt werden; die eigentliche Frischte der Darstellung, die den Leser an den Originalberichten erfreut, wird ueberwiegend verloren gehen.

L   Die Gegenwaertige Erhebung versucht festzustellen: einerseits, welche Einwirkung die geschlossene Grossindustrie auf persoenliche Eigenart, befrufliches Schicksal und ausserberuflichen "Lebenstil" ihrer Arbeiterschaft ausuebt, welche physischen und psychischen Qualitaeten sie in ihnen entwickelt, und wie sich diese in der gesamten Lebensfuerung der Arbeiterschaft aeussern,-- anderseits: inwieweit die Grossindustrie ihrerseits in ihrer Entwicklungsfaehigkeit und Entwicklungsrichtung an gegebene, durch ethnische, soziale, kulturelle Provenienz, Tradition und Lebenbedingunen der Arbeiterschaft erzeugte Qualitaeten derselben gebunden ist (Weber, 1908:1).

M   "Zur Psychophysik der industriellen Arbeit."

N "Methodologische Einleitung fuer die Erhebung des Vereins
fuer Sozialpolitik ueber Auslese und Anpassung (Berufs-
wahlen und Berufsschicksal) der Arbeiterschaft der
geschlossenen Grossindustrie."

O ...die Arbeiter ihre Leistung nach Mass und Art
plannvol zu >>materiellen<<
(d.h.: >>Erwerbs<<) Zwecken regulieren... (Weber, 1908b
in Weber, 1924a:132)

P ...der kausal interessierende Punkt, je nach dem Mass der
Fortschritte der biochemischen Kenntnisse, als Spezialfall
einer Erfahrungsregel dieser Wissenschaft begreiflich zu
machen, introspektiv nachbildbar ist aber nicht die
>>Ursache<<, sondern lediglich fuer uns nur nebensachlich
interessanter... (Weber, 1908b in 1924a:133)

Q ... die >>Gesinnung<< der Arbeiterschaft und insbesondere
ihre jewiligen Beziehungen zum Unternehmer die Leistung
beeinflussen, wird, freilich ohne exakten Nachwies, sehr
bestimmt berichtet (Weber, 1908b in 1924a:155).

R Und von diesen quantitativen Bestimmungen aus werden wir
dann zu den qualitativen uebergehen (Weber, 1910 in
1924b:440).

S ...lediglich darauf Ruecksich nimmt, dass gewisse Werte
faktisch gewertet werden, so kanr sie auch niemals
entschieden, ob eine Veraenderungsreihe ein Fortschritt oder

ein Rueckschritt ist (Rickert, 1926:95).

T Ein winziger Teil der Jeweils betrachtete individuellen Wirklichkeit wird von unserem durch jene Wertideen bedingen Interesse gefaerbt, er allein had Bedeutung fuer uns, er hat sie, weil er Beziehungen aufweist, die fuer uns infolge ihrer Verknuepfung mit Wertideen wichtig sind nur weil und soweit dies der Fall, ist er in seiner individuellen Eigenart fuer uns Wissenwert (Weber, 1924b:175).

U Simmel hat zunaechst das Verdienst, innerhalb des weitesten umkreises, den der Begriff des "Verstehens"...das objectiv "Verstehen" des Sinnes einer Auesserung von der subjectiven "Deutung" der Motive eines (sprechenden oder handlenden) Menschen klar geschieden zu haben... (Weber, 1951:93).

V Der Ausdruck "Verstehen" hat viele Bedeutungen...und die Theorien des Verstehens sind so manningfaltig, wie der Sinn des Wortes (Rickert, 1921:424).

W ...das Problem des Verstehens ist nicht psychologisch, d.h. nicht durch Erforschung des realen Seelenlebens allein zu loesen.

X Das Begriffspaar Realtypus-Idealtypus ist in der anglo-amerikanischen Literatur fast unbekannt (Machlup, 1960:54).

APPENDIX B: GLOSSARY OF TERMS

Adequate Causation   "Weaker" notion of causation taken from physiologist von Kries. The result of the "prior determination of objective possibilities" (Weber, 1949:177). Forms the basis for Erklaerendes Verstehen.

Aktuelles Verstehen   Empirical, "immediate" form of understanding. Ensures apprehension of meanings of individuals in the context of social action (Weber, 1968:275; 1978a:5,6--cf. Parsons, 1978:58n).

Comparative Method   Constitutes Weber's transition from critic of historical method to proponent of sociological research. Intended only as the initial research act; not a complete method in itself (Weber, 1914).

Cultural Values   Expressions in the social world of transcendental (also termed "universal") values, forming the initial locus of interest for the social scientist--e.g., forms of development of music; types of rationalization (Weber, 1958a; 1958b; 1975b).

Empirical Method   Employment of quantitative techniques. Weber's efforts largely unknown in American and German sociology. Weber both initiated quantitative efforts, and contributed to the refinement of forms of measurement (Weber, 1892; 1893; 1909b; 1911).

Erklaerendes Verstehen   Interpretive understanding of complex, abstract forms of behavior. Associated with the concepts of objective possibility and adequate causation. Constitutes the basis for the construction of ideal types (Weber, 1978:4--cf. Parsons, 1978:58n).

Ideal Types   Exist logically prior to the research act. Not ends of research in themselves. Also termed "ideal concepts" [Idealbildern], "conceptual constructs" [Gedankenbildern], and "pure types" [Reintypen]. Expanded the notion of Rickert's "historical individual." Establish a basis for objectivity apart from the methods of the natural sciences (Weber, 1891:266; 1949:29, 100-101; 1975a:190; 1978a:21-22).

Methodenstreit   "Crisis of method" in the social sciences. Arose partly in response to the failure of Hegelianism, partly from the uncritical domination of positivism. Weber's methodological concern arose as an attempt to resolve this crisis (Weber, 1903; 1906a; 1906b).

Objective Possibility   Abstraction that forms the basis for assessing judgments of contingency. Employed with the objective of arriving at a set of conditions capable of producing a specified event. Forms the basis for adequate causation (Weber, 1949:173-177).

Prototypes   Collection of those elements utilized in the construction of ideal types. Usually historical structures, although were often more concrete (cf. Schweitzer, 1964; Marianne Weber, 1975).

Realtypes   The concrete phenomena to which ideal types refer.   Specification of real types avoids the "process-product" fallacy of confusing ideal types and real types (cf. Euken, 1951; Machlup, 1960; Dieckmann, 1967).

Universal (transcendental) Values   Closely follows Rickert's "suprahistorical" values.   Avoids methodological relativism and limits of historical and cultural variation (Weber, 1949: 58-59--cf. Burger, 1976:41; Willey, 1978:152; Oakes, 1975:610-611).

Value Freedom   Distinct from "value-neutrality."   Enters into consideration with analysis of the problem; not a factor in its definition.   Sphere of "science" may not directly inform the sphere of "values" in any manner (Weber, 1921:21; 1949:3-50--cf. Ritzal, 1950; Bruun, 1972).

Value Interpretation   Central task of sociologists.   Object of research is not to establish values, but examine their meanings as expressed in social action.   Examination of an intention that is expressed in social action (Weber, 1949:21--cf. Bruun, 1972:36; Munch, 1975:63).

Value Judgments   "Practical evaluations of the unsatisfactory or satisfactory character of phenomena subject to [social] influence" (Weber, 1949:1; 1978c).

Value Relevance   Expressed at the object level of research. Decisive criteria for definition of any subject is concomitant with the values of the social scientist (Weber, 1968:175; 175b:57).

Werturteilstreit   "Crisis of values" in the social sciences. Debate over the incorporation of "universal" values in society by social scientists (Weber, 1907; 1949; 1968).

CONCEPTS EXPLICATED BY WEBER IN THE ESSAY,

"SOME CATEGORIES OF INTERPRETIVE SOCIOLOGY"

Adequate Causation

Conflict

Consensus and Consensual Action

   --Subtypes: Mass-conditioned action, Joint Action,

      Consensus-Conditioned Social Action

Domination (Herrschaft)

Established Order

Factually Objective Correct Rationality

Ideal Type

Institution and Institutional Action

Instrumentally rational Action

Legitimacy Consensus

Objective Meaning

Objective Possibility

   --Subtype: Average Objective Possibility

Objectively Correct Rationality

Organization and Organizational Action

Rational Social Differentiation

Status Convention

Subjective Meaning

Verstehen

Voluntary Association

BIBLIOGRAPHY

Abel, Theodore
  1929 Systematic Sociology in Germany. New York:
       Columbia University Press.

Alexander, Jeffrey C.
  1983 Theoretical Logic in Sociology, vol. 3: The
       Classical Attempt at Theoretical Synthesis--Max
       Weber. Berkeley: University of California
       Press.

Baar, Carl
  1967 "Max Weber and the Process of Social Under-
       standing." Sociology and Social Research
       51: 337-346.

Barker, Martin
  1980 "Kant as a Problem for Weber." British Journal
       of Sociology 31,2: 224-245.

Bendix, Reinhard
  1962 Max Weber: An Intellectuaul Portrait. Garden
       City, New York: Doubleday.

  1971 "Jacob Burkhardt and Max Weber." American
       Sociological Review 30,2 (April): 176-184.

Bendix, Reinhard and Guenther Roth
  1971 Scholarship and Partisanship: Essays on Max
       Weber. Berkeley: University of California Press.

Bennion, Lowell L.
  1933 Max Weber's Methodology. Paris: Le Presses
       Modernes.

Bershady, Harold
  1973 Ideology and the Development of Social
       Knowledge. New York: Wiley and Sons.

Blau, Peter and Marshall Meyer
  1971 Bureaucracy and Modern Society. New York:
       Random House.

Bogart, Robert W.
  1977 "An Assessment of Max Weber's Contribution to
       the Debate over Positivism." Sociological
       Analysis and Theory 7,1: 1-19.

Brand, M.A.
1979   "Causality, Objectivity, and Freedom: Kant,
       Weber, and the neo-Kantians." Australian and
       New Zealand Journal of Sociology 15,1: 6-12.

Bruun, H.H.
1972   Science, Values, and Politics in Max Weber's
       Methodology. Copenhagen: Munksgaard.

Burger, Thomas
1976   Max Weber's Theory of Concept Formation: History,
       Laws, and Ideal Types. Durham, North Carolina:
       Duke University Press.

1977   "Max Weber's Interpretive Sociology, and the
       Sense of Historical Science: A Positivistic
       Conception of Verstehen." The Sociological
       Quarterly 18 (Spring): 165-175.

Butts, Stewart
1977   "Parsons' Interpretation of Weber: A Methodological
       Analysis." Sociological Analysis and Theory
       7,3: 227-241.

Cahnman, Werner
1979   "Review of Seyfarth, Constans and Gert Schmidt."
       Max Weber Bibliographie: Eine Dokumentation der
       Sekundaerliterature. Stuttgart: Ferdinand
       Enke Verlag, 1977.

Collins, Randall
1975   Conflict Sociology: Toward an Explanatory
       Science. New York: Academic Press.

1980   "Weber's Last Theory of Capitialism." American
       Sociological Review 45,6 (Dec.): 925-942.

Coser, Lewis A.
1971   Masters of Sociological Thought. New York: Harcourt
       Brace Janovich.

Diamant, Alfred
1962   "The Bureaucratic Model: Max Weber Rejected,
       Rediscovered, Reformed." In: Ferrel Heady
       and Sybil L. Stokes (eds)> Papers in Compara-
       tive Public Administration. Ann Arbor: Uni-
       versity of Michigan Press.

Elias, Norbert
1982   "Soziologie in Gefaehr: Plaedoyer fuer die Neu-
       orientierung einer Wissenschaft." Suddeutsche
       Zeitung, 233 (Oct. 9-10): 107.

Eliaeson, Sven
  1971 "Some Recent Interpretations of Max Weber's
         Methodology.: Sociological Analysis and
         Theory 7,1: 21-71.

Euken, Walter
  1951 The Foundations of Economics. Chicago: University
         of Chicago Press.

Fleischmann, Eugene
  1964 "De Weber a' Nietzsche." Archives Europeen de
         Soziologie 5: 190-238.

Freund, Julian
  1968 The Sociology of Max Weber (trans. Mary Ilford).
         New York: Pantheon.

Gerth, Hans and C. Wright Mills
  1975 "Introduction." In Max Weber, From Max Weber.
         New York: Oxford.

Giddens, Anthony
  1971 Capitalism and Modern Social Theory. London:
         Cambridge.

Gibbs, Jack
  1966 Sociological Theory Construction. New York:
         Random House.

Gilbert, Dennis
  1976 "Social Values and Social Science: An Examination
         of the Methodological Writings of Weber and Durkheim."
         Cornell Journal of Social Relations 11,1: 23-29.

Graber, Edith
  1981 "Translator's Introduction to Max Weber's Essay on
         Some Categories of Interpretive Sociology."
         Sociological Quarterly 22 (Spring): 145-150.

Habermas, Juergen
  1971 Toward a Rational Society (trans. Jeremy Shapiro).
         London: Heinemann.

Heckmann, Friedrich
  1979 "Max Weber als empirischer Sozialforscher."
         Zeitschrift fuer Soziologie 8,1: 50:62.

Henrich, Dieter
  1952 Die Einheit der Wissenschaft Max Webers. Tuebingen:
         Mohr-Siebeck.

Heuss, Alfred
1965 "Max Weber's Bedeutung fuer die Geschichte des
griechisch-roemischen Altertums." Historische
Zeitschrift 201,3 (Dez.): 529-556.

Hodges, H.A.
1949 Wilhelm Dilthey. London: Routledge and Kegan Paul.

Horkheimer, Max
1973 Eclipse of Reason. New York: Continuum.

Kaesler, Dirk
1979 Einfuehrung in das Studium Max Webers. Muenchen:
Beck.

Kaufmann, Walter
1976 Existentialism from Dostoevsky to Sartre.
Glencoe: The Free Press.

Lazarsfeld, Paul F. and Anthony R. Oberschall
1965 "Max Weber and Empirical Social Research."
American Sociological Review 30,2: 185-198.

Leat, Diana
1972 "Misunderstanding Verstehen." The Sociological
Review 30,2: 185-198.

Lewis, John
1975 Max Weber and Value-free Sociology. London:
Lawrence and Wishart.

Loewith, Karl
1970 "Max Weber and Karl Marx." In Dennis
Wrong, ed. Max Weber. Englewood Cliffs: Prentice-Hall.

Lopreato, Joseph and Leticia Alston
1970 "Ideal Types and the Idealization Strategy."
American Sociological Review 35,1 (Feb.): 88-96.

Lorenzen, Paul
1970 "Enlightenment and Reason." Continuum 18 (Summer): 3-11.

Machlup, Fritz
1960 "Idealtypus, Wirklichkeit, und Konstruction."
Ordo: Jahrbuch fuer die Ordnung von Wirtschaft
und Gesellschaft: 21-57.

Marcuse, Herbert
1968 Negations: Essays in Critical Theory. Boston:
Beacon.

Markovic, Mahailo
  1972 "The Problem of Reification and the Verstehen-
        Erklaeren Controversy." Acta Sociologica
        15: 27-38.

Martindale, Don
  1959 "Sociological Theory and the Ideal Type." In
        L. Gross (ed). Symposium on Sociological Theory.
        New York: Harper and Row, pp. 57-81.

Menger, Carl
  1883 Untersuchen ueber die Methode der Sozialwissenschaften
        und der politischen Oekonomie insbesondere. Leipzig.

Mommsen, Wolfgang
  1959 Max Weber und die deutsche
        Politik, 1890-1920. Tuebingen: Mohr-Siebeck.

  1977a The Age of Bureaucracy: Perspectives of the
        Political Sociology of Max Weber. New York:
        Harper.

  1977b "Max Weber as Critic of Marxism." Canadian
        Journal of Sociology 13,3: 373-398.

Mueller, G.H.
  1979 "The Notion of Rationality in the Work of
        Max Weber." Archives Europeenes de Sociologie
        20: 149-171.

Munch, Peter A.
  1975 "'Sense' and 'Intention' in Max Weber's Theory
        of Social Action." Sociological Inquiry 45,4: 59-65.

Nelson, Benjamin
  1975 "Ernst Troeltsch, Georg Jellinek, and Max Weber
        as Comparative Historical Sociologists." Socio-
        logical Analysis 36,3: 229-240.

Oakes, Guy
  1975 "Introductory Essay to Max Weber, Essays on
        Roscher and Knies: The Logical Problems of
        Historical Economics." New York: Free Press.

  1982 "Methodological Ambivalence: The Case of Max
        Weber." Social Research 49,3: 589-615.

Oberschall, Anthony
  1965 Empirical Social Science Research in Germany,
        1848-1914. Paris: Mouton.

Parsons, Talcott
1949   The Structure of Social Action.   New York:
       Free Press.

Ritzer, George
1975   "Sociology: A Multiple Paradigm Science." Amer-
       ican Sociologist 45: 85-97.

Robertson, Roland
1975   "On the Analysis of Mysticism: Pre-Weberian,
       Weberian, and Post-Weberian Perspectives."
       Sociological Analysis 36,3: 241-266.

Roth, Guenther
1968   "Translator's Introduction to Max Weber, Economy
       and Society. Berkeley: University of California
       Press.

1975   "Survey Review." Contemporary Sociology 4,4
       (July): 367-373.

Roth, Guenther and Wolfgang Schluchter
1979   Max Weber's Vision of History. Berkeley:
       University of California Press.

Runciman, W. G
1972   A Critique of Max Weber's Philosophy of
       Social Action. Cambridge: Cambridge Universtiy
       Press.

Schluchter, Wolfgang
1971   Wertfreiheit und Verantwortungsethik. Tuebingen:
       Mohr.

1979   The Rise of Western Rationalism. Berkeley: University
       of California Press.

Schuetz, Alfred
1967   The Phenomenology of the Social World (trans. George
       Walsh and Frederick Lennert). Northwestern
       University Press.

Schmoller, Gustav
1883   "Zur Methodologie der Staats- und Sozialwissenschaften."
       Schmollers Jahrbuch fuer Gesetzgebung, Verwaltung, und
       Volkswirtschaft: 239-258.

Schweitzer, Arthur
1964   "Vom Idealtypus zum Prototyp." Zietschrift fuer
       die Gesamte Staatswissenschaft 120,1: 56-64.

Seyfarth, Constans and Gert Schmidt
    1977   Max Weber Bibliographie: Eine Dokumentation
           der Sekundaerliteratur. Stuttgart: Ferdinand
           Enke Verlag.

Shils, Edward
    1949   "Forward to Max Weber's The Methodology of the
           Social Sciences." Glencoe: Free Press.

Sprondel, Walter M. et al.
    1980   "Soziologie soll heissen: Einige Anmerkungen zur
           Weber-Rezeption aus Anlass des 60. Geburtstages
           von Johannes Winckelmann." Koelner Zeitschrift
           fuer Soziologie und Sozialpsychologie 32,1: 1-11.

Stammer, Otto (ed).
    1965   Max Weber und die Soziologie heute. Verbandungen
           des 15. deutschen Sociologentages. Tuebingen:
           Mohr-Siebeck.

Strauss, Leo
    1953   Natural Right and History. Chicago: University
           of Chicago Press.

Tenbruck, Friedrich
    1959   "Die Genesis der Methodologie Max Webers."
           Koelner Zeitschrift fuer Soziologie und Sozial-
           pyschologie 11: 573-630.

Turner, Stephen
    1983   "Weber on Action." American Sociological Review
           29,1: 5-29.

Warriner, Charles K.
    1969   "Social Action, Behavior, and Verstehen." The
           Sociological Quarterly 10: 501-511.

Wax, Murray L.
    1967   "On Misunderstanding Verstehen: A Reply to
           Abel." Sociology and Social Research 51: 323-333.

Weber, Marianne
    1975   Max Weber: A Biography (trans. Harry Zohn). New
           York: John Wiley and Sons.

Weber, Max
    1889   Zur Geschichte der Handelsgesellschaften im
           Mittelalter. Stuttgart: Enke.

    1891   Die Roemische Agrargeschichte und ihrer Bedeutung
           fuer das Staats- und Privatrecht. Stuttgart: Enke.

1892   Die Lage der Landarbeiter im ostelbischen Deutsch-
        land. Schriften des Vereins fuer Sozialpolitik,
        volume 3.

1893a   "Die Erhebungen des Evangelisch-Sozialen Kongresses
        ueber die Verhaeltnesse der Landarbeiter Deutsch-
        lands." Christliche Welt: 535-540.

1893b   "Referat: die landliche Arbeitsverfassung."
        Schriften des Vereins fuer Sozialpolitik 58: 62-86.

1895   "Antrittsrede: Der Nationalstaat und die Volks-
        wirtschaftspolitik." Tuebingen: J.C.B. Mohr.

1896   "Die socialen Gruende des Untergangs der antiken
        Kultur." Die Wahrheit. Halbmonatschrift zur
        Vertiefung in die Fragen und Aufgaben des
        Menschenlebens 6,3 (May): 57-77.

1909a   "Letter to Heinrich Rickert," April 2.
        Max Weber Archives: Bavarian Academy of Social
        Sciences, Munich.

1949   The Methodology of the Social Sciences (trans.
        Edward A. Shils and Henry A. Finch.) New York:
        Free Press.

1968   Gesammelte Aufsaetze zur Wissenschaftslehre.
        Tuebingen: Mohr-Siebeck.

1975b   Essays on Roscher and Knies: The Logical Problems
        of Historical Economics (trans. Guy Oakes). New
        York: Free Press.

1978a   Economy and Society (trans. Guenther Roth et al).
[1922] Berkeley: University of California Press.

1978b   "The Nature of Social Action." Pp. 7-42 in W.G.
[1922] Runciman (ed). Weber: Selections in Translation
        (trans. Gary Matthews). New York: Cambridge
        University Press.

1978c   "Value Judgements in Social Science. In W.G.
[1917]   Runciman (ed). Weber: Selections in Translation
        (trans. Gary Matthews). New York: Cambridge
        University Press.

Whitehead, Alfred North
    1959   The Aims of Education and Other Essays. New
           York: Macmillan.

Winckelmann, Johannes (ed).
  1964 Max Weber. Soziologie--Weltgeschichte Analyse--
        Politik. Stuttgart: Kroner.

Zeitlin, Irving
  1973 Rethinking Sociology: A Critique of Contemporary
        Theory. New York: Appleton-Century-Crofts.

INDEX

Abel, T., 2, 19, 101, 108, 109, 123, 130
Adequate Causation, 72, 82, 83, 95-99, 102
Aktuelles Verstehen, 84, 110, 122-125, 130, 136, 143
Alexander, J., 8
Alston, L. 19, 112
Anschaulichkeit, 47
Antonio R., 89
Antrittsrede, (Weber's), 34, 35, 61
Aron, R., 112
Ascetic rationalism, 137
Axiological foundation of the sciences, 53, 81

Baar, C., 19, 103
Baden School of neo-Kantianism, 18, 44-45, 54, 77, 129
Barker, M. 8, 18
Baumgarten, E. 75
Bendix, R. 8, 9, 14, 15, 19, 23, 32, 33
Bennion, L. 2, 88
Bershady, H., 6
Blau, P., 19, 115
Bogart, R., 1, 2, 8
Brand, M., 8, 9, 89
Brubaker, R., 134
Bruun, H.H., 2, 6, 8, 11, 12, 13, 14, 16, 17, 19, 23, 25,
    34, 35, 57, 81, 92, 93, 121
Bureaucracy, 83, 137, 141, 142
Bureaucratization, 26
Burger, T., 2, 8, 11, 12, 16, 17, 19, 39, 44, 47, 48, 49,
    52, 55, 77, 86, 94, 101, 103, 108, 113
Butts, S., 2, 6, 89

Cahnman, W., 1
Calvinism, 135
Capitalism: incipient, 26, 27; modern, 26; transition to
    modern capitalism, 30
Categorical Imperative, 44
Causality, 96, 98
Cerny, C. 11
Charismatic leaders, 27
Classical School of economics, 56
Cohen, H., 43

Collins, R., 1, 8
Comparative method, 27, 78, 83, 118
Concept formation, 77
Contractual labor, 30
Copy theory of knowledge, 49
Coser, L., 8
Cultural values, 12, 32, 81, 82, 87-90
"Cumulative science" argument, 5-10

Dahrendorff, R., 57
Dampier, 41
Decisionism, 5, 10, 128
Decisionist critique, 10-13
Democratization, 26
Diamant, A., 19
Dieckmann, J., 89, 112, 113
Dilthey, W., 8, 47, 48, 91, 103, 105, 130
Durkheim, E., 139, 141

Economic development, 12
Economic history, 26
Economic irrationality, 66
Economic motives, 32, 33
Economic policy, 11, 34
Egypt, 119
Elias, N., 10
Eliason, S., 25
Emanatism, 28
Empirical Types, 83, 110-116, 142
Empirical Typologies, 36
Erklaerendes Verstehen, 83, 109-110, 122, 130, 137, 142
Ethic of responsibility, 94
Eudaemonistic principles, 93
Eudaemonistic value theory, 51
Euken, W., 19
Evangelical-Social Congress, 32
Extensive infinity: of social reality, 90; of cultural
  values, 82

Ferrarotti, F., 93, 109, 110
Feudalism, 30, 31
Fleischmann, E., 8
Freund, J., 21, 54, 55, 90

Geisteswissenschaften, 47, 48

Generalizing approach (to knowledge), 46
Germanic law, 26
German Sociological Association, 57
German workers, 31
Gerth, H., 1, 8, 14, 88, 121, 134
Gibbs, J., 6, 7
Giddens, A., 6, 8, 42
Gilbert, D., 3, 17
Goddard, D., 54
Graber, E., 14, 24, 70, 71, 79
Greece, 119
Gutherrschaft, system of, 30

Habermas, J., 10, 11
Habilitationsschrift (Weber's), 25, 128, 129
Habitual action, 75
Heckmann, F., 3, 17, 23, 33, 67, 93
Hegelian idealism, 40
Hegelianism, 40, 41
Hekman, S., 110, 114
Helle, H., 93, 106
Hellenic realm, 119
Henrich, D., 23, 24, 47
Heuss, A., 29
Historical data, 69
Historical determinism, 46, 56
Historical equivalents, 24, 78
Historical materialism, 9
Historical school, 39
Historical sciences, 41
Historicism, 9
History of sociology, 4
Hodges, E., 8, 105
Honigsheim, P., 58
Horkheimer, M., 10
Hospers, J., 64
Howe, R., 93
Huff, T., 2
Hughes, H., 105
Humanistic rationalism, 157
Husserl, E., 91

Idiographic sciences, 46, 95
Ideal type: critiques of 19; Weber's initial formulation
   of, 28, 109; and empirical types, 83, 110-116; and
   prototypes, 82, 110-116; as descriptive mechanisms,
   73; and economic phenomena, 69; Rickert's influence
   on Weber's concept of, 54
Idealbildern, 28

Idealschemen, 29, 78
Iggers, G., 6, 43, 44, 50, 52, 54, 85, 105
Imperial Rome, 119
Incipient capitalism, 27
Individualizing approach (to knowledge), 46
Instrumental rationality, 13, 124, 143
Instrumentally rational action, 71, 75, 136, 137
Intensive infinity of cultural values, 82
Intentionality, 96
Interpretation, problems of, 13-16
Interpretive sociology, 24, 59, 73
Intersubjective understanding, 65, 124
Intuitionism, 43, 103-104, 106, 122
Intuitionists, 54, 70

Jaffe, E., 57
Jaspers, K., 74
Jellinek, G., 8
Junkers, 13, 30

Kaesler, D., 1, 9, 13, 22, 27, 29, 52
Kalberg, S., 90
Kamenka, G., 40
Kant, I., 8, 17, 50, 51
Kantian, 87, 133
Kantian dualism, 93
Kaufman, W., 6
Knies, K., 56
Kulturwissenschaft, 48

Lazarsfeld, P., 19, 22, 32, 33, 63, 67, 123
Leat, D., 19, 93
Leff, G., 105
Legal history, 26
Levenstein, A., 67, 68
Lewis, J., 12
Loewith, K., 8
Lopreato, J., 19, 112
Lorenzen, P., 8

Machlup, F., 19, 109, 115
Marathon, Battle of, 97
Marburg School of neo-Kantianism, 43, 44
Marcuse, H., 10
Markovic, M., 19. 101

Martindale, D., 8, 42, 48, 73, 117
Marx, K., 8, 56, 109
Marxists, 9
Meaning, two types of, 75
Menger, C., 56
Mesopotamia, 119
Methodenstreit, 17, 22, 39-59, 103, 129
Methodological individualism, 75
Meyer, E., 56
Meyer, M., 19
Mills, C.W., 8, 14, 88, 121, 134
Mommsen, W., 8, 9, 10, 24, 35
Moon, D., 101
Moore, W., 134
Moscow, 120
Mueller, 6, 8
Munch, P., 19, 93 101

Nacherleben, 104
naive positivism, 11, 130
Natorp, P., 43
Nelson, B., 8, 19, 118
Neo-Hegelians, 8, 9
Neo-Idealism, 90
Neo-Kantian(s), 18, 22, 72, 85, 86, 105, 113, 131
Neo-Kantianism, 42-55, 81
Natural science method, 41, 45, 46, 48, 51, 52, 53, 54,
    64, 66, 96, 102
Naturwissenschaften, 47, 48
Nietzsche, F., 8, 9, 13
Nomological science, 41, 46, 52

Oakes, G., 3, 8, 10, 13, 14, 17, 19, 22, 40, 41, 44, 44,
    52, 55, 72, 87, 91, 121
Oberschall, A., 19, 22, 23, 32, 33, 63, 64, 66, 67, 69,
    121, 123
Object level of values (in research), 81, 91, 133
Objective meanings, 54
Objective possibility, 72, 82, 83, 95-99, 102
Objectively "correct" meanings, 53
Objectivity of the social sciences, 43, 50
Organic positivism, 73, 78, 102, 103

Parsons, T., 1, 17, 42, 77, 112, 118, 122
Patrimonialism, 27
Peking, 120
Phenomenologists, 74, 123
Phenomenology, 78

Philosophy of history, 50
Plato, 90
Polish workers, 13, 30
Positivism, 41
Positivists, 58
Practical reason, 43
Progress, as a value, 49, 82, 88
Prototypes, 83, 110-116, 142
Prussia, 13, 30, 34
Psycho-physical variables, 64-66
Pure reason, 43
Pure types, 53
Pythagoras, 90

Randall, J., 41
Rational conduct, 53, 65
Rationality, 43, 64, 72, 81, 82, 89, 90, 134-138, 142-143
Rationalization, 90, 137, 142
Reintyp, 53
Relativism, 41, 49, 86, 87, 131
Republican Rome, 119
Research: Weber's initial attempts, 21-37, 52; failures
    of, 22-23, 33; Weber's contributions to, 23, 24, 26,
    32-33, 62, 67, 67
Research level of values, 81, 91, 133
Revolution of 1848, 40
Rex, J., 106, 116, 118
Rickert, H., 18, 24, 44, 47-52, 54, 55, 74, 75, 85, 86,
    88, 90, 92, 101, 103, 107, 138
Ritzer, G., 8, 112, 121
Robertson, R., 8
Roman agriculture, 27
Roman expansionism, 111
Roman law, 26
Roscher, W., 56
Roth, G., 1, 2, 3, 8, 9, 10, 13, 14, 19, 25, 26, 27, 33,
    70, 89, 117
Rules of experience, 83, 97, 109, 115
Runciman, W., 1, 19
Runes, D., 90

Sahay, A., 113, 133, 138
Salomon, E., 112
Scientism, 41
von Schelting, A., 102, 128
Schluchter, W., 3, 8, 10, 11, 12, 89, 94
Schmidt, C., 11
von Schmoller, G., 18, 39, 56, 57
Schneider, L., 55

Schuetz, A., 1, 123
Schweitzer, W., 19
Shils, E., 2
Simmel, G., 53, 74, 103, 105-107, 129, 139
Social Democrats, 67
Sprondel, W., 3
Stammler, R., 56
Strauss, L., 1
Subjective meaning, 53, 54, 130
Subjective states of individuals, 65, 128

Taylorism, 64
Tenbruck, F., 3, 24, 25, 35, 77, 89, 113
Theodorson, G., 85
Toennies, F., 8, 9
Torrance, J., 2
Translation, problems of, 13-16
Troeltsch, E., 8, 18
Truzzi, M., 130
Turner, B., 138
Turner, S., 8, 96, 98
Typological construction, 68
Typologies, 68

Udehn, L., 134
Universalistic method, 75
Universal values, 12, 81, 86-87, 133

Vaihinger, L., 113
Vallier, I., 118
Value-freedom, 10, 12, 29, 34, 57, 63, 69, 78, 81
Value-ideas, 91
Value-interpretation, 12, 81, 92-95
Value-judgements, 12, 81, 84, 86, 92-95, 131
Value-relation (Rickert), 48
Value-relativity, 90-92
Value-relevance, 12, 72, 75, 78, 92-95, 102, 107
Values: in Weber's works, 10, 13, 28, 31, 33-34; as
  distinct from science, 27, 34, 36, relation of
  values to science, 35-36, 81; "asymmetrical" and
  "symmetrical" relationships of science to values, 35-36,
    81; ontological and axiological status of, 43, 81;
  in the social sciences, 55, 58, 85-95; types of, 86, 94;
  hierarchy of, 81;
Verein fuer Sozialpolitik, 18, 29, 31, 57, 62, 67, 68,
  69, 128
Verstehen, 16, 78, 101-110; critiques of, 19, Weber's

concept as opposed to other formulations, 105-107; as
  interpretive understanding, 54, 70, 71
"Verstehende" sociology, 75
Volksgeist, 56
Volkswohlstand, 35

Wage labor, 30
Warriner, C., 19, 101, 108
Wax, M., 19, 101, 130
Weber, Alfred, 62
Weber, Marianne, 7, 8, 14, 22, 44, 47, 54, 77, 89, 115
Werturteilstreit, 11, 22, 39-59, 61, 62, 129
Whitehead, A.N., 5
Willey, T., 40, 41, 44, 47, 48, 51, 54, 86, 93
Winch, P., 130
Winckelmann, J., 1, 24, 70
Windelband, W., 18, 44, 45-47, 52, 54, 138

Zeitlin, I., 8, 88

DATE DUE

DEC 28 '89